T0189535

Communications
in Computer and Information Science

2000

Rationale

The CCIS series is devoted to the publication of proceedings of computer science conferences. Its aim is to efficiently disseminate original research results in informatics in printed and electronic form. While the focus is on publication of peer-reviewed full papers presenting mature work, inclusion of reviewed short papers reporting on work in progress is welcome, too. Besides globally relevant meetings with internationally representative program committees guaranteeing a strict peer-reviewing and paper selection process, conferences run by societies or of high regional or national relevance are also considered for publication.

Topics

The topical scope of CCIS spans the entire spectrum of informatics ranging from foundational topics in the theory of computing to information and communications science and technology and a broad variety of interdisciplinary application fields.

Information for Volume Editors and Authors

Publication in CCIS is free of charge. No royalties are paid, however, we offer registered conference participants temporary free access to the online version of the conference proceedings on SpringerLink (http://link.springer.com) by means of an http referrer from the conference website and/or a number of complimentary printed copies, as specified in the official acceptance email of the event.

CCIS proceedings can be published in time for distribution at conferences or as post-proceedings, and delivered in the form of printed books and/or electronically as USBs and/or e-content licenses for accessing proceedings at SpringerLink. Furthermore, CCIS proceedings are included in the CCIS electronic book series hosted in the SpringerLink digital library at http://link.springer.com/bookseries/7899. Conferences publishing in CCIS are allowed to use Online Conference Service (OCS) for managing the whole proceedings lifecycle (from submission and reviewing to preparing for publication) free of charge.

Publication process

The language of publication is exclusively English. Authors publishing in CCIS have to sign the Springer CCIS copyright transfer form, however, they are free to use their material published in CCIS for substantially changed, more elaborate subsequent publications elsewhere. For the preparation of the camera-ready papers/files, authors have to strictly adhere to the Springer CCIS Authors' Instructions and are strongly encouraged to use the CCIS LaTeX style files or templates.

Abstracting/Indexing

CCIS is abstracted/indexed in DBLP, Google Scholar, EI-Compendex, Mathematical Reviews, SCImago, Scopus. CCIS volumes are also submitted for the inclusion in ISI Proceedings.

How to start

To start the evaluation of your proposal for inclusion in the CCIS series, please send an e-mail to ccis@springer.com.

Ramesh C. Bansal · Margarita N. Favorskaya ·
Shahbaz Ahmed Siddiqui · Pooja Jain ·
Ankush Tandon
Editors

Advanced Computing Techniques in Engineering and Technology

First International Conference, ACTET 2023
Jaipur, India, December 18–19, 2023
Proceedings

 Springer

Editors
Ramesh C. Bansal 🆔
University of Sharjah
Sharjah, United Arab Emirates

University of Pretoria
Pretoria, South Africa

Shahbaz Ahmed Siddiqui 🆔
Manipal University Jaipur
Jaipur, Rajasthan, India

Ankush Tandon 🆔
Swami Keshvanand Institute of Technology
Management and Gramothan
Jaipur, Rajasthan, India

Margarita N. Favorskaya 🆔
Reshetnev Siberian State University
of Science and Technology Krasnoyarsk
Krasnoyarsk, Russia

Pooja Jain 🆔
Swami Keshvanand Institute of Technology
Management and Gramothan
Jaipur, Rajasthan, India

ISSN 1865-0929   ISSN 1865-0937 (electronic)
Communications in Computer and Information Science
ISBN 978-3-031-54161-2   ISBN 978-3-031-54162-9 (eBook)
https://doi.org/10.1007/978-3-031-54162-9

This Springer imprint is published by the registered company Springer Nature Switzerland AG
The registered company address is: Gewerbestrasse 11, 6330 Cham, Switzerland

Paper in this product is recyclable.

Preface

The Conference on Advanced Computing Techniques in Engineering & Technology (ACTET 2023) was an International Conference organized with publication support from Springer. It was organized by the Department of Electrical Engineering, Swami Keshvanand Institute of Technology Management & Gramothan, Jaipur, Rajasthan, India, with technical sponsorship from the Soft Computing Research Society (SCRS).

With the advent of high-performance computing environments, virtualization, distributed and parallel computing, as well as increasing memory, storage and computational power, processing particularly complex scientific applications and voluminous data is more affordable. With the current computing software, hardware and distributed platforms effective use of advanced computing techniques is more achievable. The goal of the International Conference on Advanced Computing Techniques in Engineering & Technology (ACTET 2023) was to bring together researchers from academia and practitioners from industry in order to address the fundamentals of advanced scientific computing and specific mechanisms and algorithms in particular and to exchange their innovative ideas, knowledge, expertise and experience in advanced computing techniques in various domains of engineering and technology.

The conference provided a forum where researchers were able to present recent research results and new research problems and directions related to them. The conference sought contributions presenting novel research in all aspects of new scientific methods for computing and hybrid methods for computing optimization, as well as advanced algorithms and computational procedures, software and hardware solutions dealing with specific domains of science such as Electrical and Electronics Engineering.

On behalf of Swami Keshvanand Institute of Technology Management & Gramothan, we are pleased to welcome all readers to the Proceedings of the International Conference on Advanced Computing Techniques in Engineering & Technology (ACTET 2023). This conference provided an environment to conduct intellectual discussions and exchange ideas that will be instrumental in shaping the future of Computing Techniques. It was planned in two tracks, viz. Track 1: Advanced Computing Techniques, and Track 2: Application Areas for Advanced Computing Techniques, and one Special session on Micro and Nano-electronic Circuits and Systems. The conference got a very good response from across India and other countries.

A total of 89 papers were submitted for review in a single-blind process, and these underwent evaluation by various reviewers from esteemed institutions across India and abroad. Each paper underwent scrutiny from three reviewers to ensure a comprehensive and fair assessment. A total of 7 papers were accepted for presentation at the conference, and presented during December 18–19, 2023.

February 2024

Ramesh C. Bansal
Margarita N. Favorskaya
Shahbaz Ahmed Siddiqui
Pooja Jain
Ankush Tandon

Organization

Executive Program Chairs

Raja Ram Meel, Patron   SKIT M&G, Jaipur, India
Surja Ram Meel, Chairman SKIT M&G, Jaipur, India
S. L. Surana, Director   SKIT M&G, Jaipur, India
 (Academics)

General Chairs

Ramesh C. Bansal   University of Sharjah, UAE
Ramesh Kumar Pachar SKIT M&G, Jaipur, India

Program Committee Chairs

Ramesh C. Bansal   University of Sharjah, UAE
Margarita N. Favorskaya Reshetnev Siberian State University of Science
            and Technology, Russian Federation
Shahbaz Ahmed Siddiqui Manipal University Jaipur, India
Pooja Jain   SKIT M&G, Jaipur, India
Ankush Tandon   SKIT M&G, Jaipur, India

Conference Chairs

Nilanjan Dey   Techno International New Town, India
Richi Nayak   Queensland University of Technology, Australia
Shahbaz Ahmed Siddiqui Manipal University, Jaipur, India

Technical Program Chairs

Margarita N. Favorskaya Reshetnev Siberian State University of Science
            and Technology, Russian Federation
Ameena Al Sumaiti   Khalifa University, UAE
Ankush Tandon   SKIT M&G, Jaipur, India

Pooja Jain   SKIT M&G, Jaipur, India

Organizing Chairs

Basant Agarwal	Central University of Rajasthan, India
Md. Rizwan	DTU, Delhi, India
Sarfaraz Nawaz	SKIT M&G, Jaipur, India

Publication Chairs

Neeraj Gupta	Oakland University, USA
Bhanu Pratap Soni	Fiji National University, Fiji
Kapil Shukla	MNIT, Jaipur, India
Divya Rishi Shrivastava	Manipal University Jaipur, India
Rishi Vyas	SKIT M&G, Jaipur, India

Finance Chairs

Ajay Kumar	PEC, Chandigarh, India
Ankit Agarwal	SKIT M&G, Jaipur, India
Vikas Ranveer Singh Mahala	SKIT M&G, Jaipur, India

Publicity Chairs

Mehul Mahrishi	Writing Lab, USA
Manish Rawat	Manipal University Jaipur, India
Rukhsar Zafar	SKIT M&G, Jaipur, India
Naveen Jain	SKIT M&G, Jaipur, India

Organizing Secretaries

Akanksha Shukla	SVNIT, Surat, India
Prateek Singhal	SKIT M&G, Jaipur, India
Deepti Arela	SKIT M&G, Jaipur, India
Naveen Kumar Sain	SKIT M&G, Jaipur, India

Conference Coordinators

Ankush Tandon	SKIT M&G, Jaipur, India
Pooja Jain	SKIT M&G, Jaipur, India

Advisory Board

Ramesh C. Bansal	University of Sharjah, UAE
A. G. Hessami	Vega Systems, UK
Richi Nayak	Queensland University of Technology, Australia
Margarita N. Favorskaya	Reshetnev Siberian State University of Science and Technology, Russian Federation
Hasmat Malik	UTM, Malaysia
Bhanu Pratap Soni	Fiji National University, Fiji
Md. Khalid Imam Rahmani	Saudi Electronic University, Saudi Arabia
Ramkrishan Maheshwari	University of Southern Denmark, Denmark
Ameena Al-Sumaiti	Khalifa University, UAE
Smaranda Belciug	University of Craiova, Romania
Larisa	Politehnica University of Timisoara, Romania
Nilanjan Dey	Techno International New Town, India
Jagdish Chand Bansal	South Asian University, India
Dheerak K Khatod	IIT BHU, India
S. P. Singh	IIT BHU, India
R. K. Pandey	IIT BHU, India
Bharat Singh	IIT Mandi, India
K. R. Niazi	MNIT Jaipur, India
Rajesh Kumar	MNIT Jaipur, India
Veena Sharma	NIT Hamirpur, India
Mahiraj Singh Rawat	NIT Uttarakhand, India
Kushal Jagtap	NIT Srinagar, India
Rajiv Tiwari	MNIT Jaipur, India
Dipti Saxena	MNIT Jaipur, India
Akanksha Shukla	SVNIT, Surat, India
Ajay Kumar	BIT Mesra, India
H. D. Mathur	BITS Pilani, India
Mahendra Lalwani	RTU, India
Ikbal Ali	Jamia Millia Islamia, India
Sheeraz Kirmani	AMU, India
Vivek Prakash	Banasthali Vidyapith, India

Technical Program Committee

Aarti Chugh	SGT University, India
Abhinav Bhatnagar	Birla Institute of Applied Sciences, India
Akanksha Shukla	SVNIT, Surat, India
Akhlaqur Rahman	Engineering Institute of Technology, Australia
Amit Gupta	GGITS, India
Amit Sharma	Career Point University, Kota, India
Anamika Yadav	National Institute of Technology, Raipur, India
Ankita	Pranveer Singh Institute of Technology, Kanpur, India
Ankush Koli	Malaviya National Institute of Technology, Jaipur, India
Anubhav Pandey	Manipal Institute of Higher Education, India
Arvind Kumar	Government Engineering College Bikaner, India
Ashwani Yadav	Amity University Jaipur, India
Awanish Mishra	Pranveer Singh Institute of Technology, Kanpur, India
Bhanu Tekwani	VIT Mumbai, India
Binod Kumar	IIT Jodhpur, India
Dhiraj Magare	Ramrao Adik Institute of Technology, India
Divya Rishi Shrivastava	Manipal University Jaipur, India
Fareed Ahmad	SND College of Engineering and Research Center, India
Ganesh Gupta	Sharda University, India
Gargi Khanna	NIT, Hamirpur, India
Garima Nahar	S. S. Jain Subodh P.G. Mahila Mahavidyalaya, India
Gaurav Jain	Poornima College of Engineering, India
Gaurav Meena	Central University of Rajasthan
H. Manoj Gadiyar	SDM Institute of Technology, India
Habib Ur Rahman Habib	Durham University, UK
Hossein Khorramdel	Shiraz University of Technology, Iran
Jyoti Bhonsle	Academic Researcher
Kapil Shukla	MNIT Jaipur, India
Karthick Prasad Gunasekaran	Amazon, USA
Kasturi Vasudevan	IIT Kanpur, India
Kaviyarasi R.	Sri Vidya Mandir Arts and Science College, India
Kevin Joshi	Respirer Living Sciences Pvt. Ltd., India
Khushboo Tripathi	Amity University Gurgaon, India
Kirti Pal	GBU, India
Mahendra Bhadu	Government Engineering College Bikaner, India

Manish Singla	Chitkara University, India
Mohit Saxena	Tata Consultancy Services, India
Monika Goyal	Dayanand Sagar University, India
Mushtaq Ahmed	MNIT Jaipur, India
Nagendra Singh	National Institute of Technology, Harimpur, India
Navin Paliwal	Govt. Engineering College, Bikaner, India
Neeraj Gupta	Amity University Haryana, India
Neeraj Kanwar	Manipal University Jaipur, India
Neha Adhikari	Central Power Research Institute, India
Nidish Vashistha	Micron Technology Inc., USA
Nikita Jain	Poornima College of Engineering, India
Nitesh Mudgal	Poornima College of Engineering, India
Parameswaran Ramesh	Madras Institute of Technology, India
Pardha Saradhi J.	Bapatla Engineering College, India
Patel Pravinbhai	Energy Systems Engineering
Praful Nandankar	Government College of Engineering, Nagpur, India
Prashant Kumar	J C Bose University of Science & Technology, India
Pravin Sonwane	Poornima College of Engineering, India
Preeti Narooka	Manipal University Jaipur, India
Prerak Bhardwaj	Jaipur Engineering College and Research Centre, India
Priyanka Makkar	Amity University Haryana, India
Radhakrishna Bhat	Manipal Institute of Technology, Manipal, India
Rahul Soni	Pandit Deendayal Energy University, India
Rajat Verma	Pranveer Singh Institute of Technology, India
Rakesh Choudhary	Swami Keshvanand Institute of Technology, Management & Gramothan, India
Rashmi Gupta	Amity University Haryana, India
Ravita Lamba	MNIT, Jaipur, India
Rudranarayan Senapati	Kalinga Institute of Industrial Technology, India
Sandeep Vyas	JECRC University, India
Sangeeta Singh	Vardhaman College of Engineering, India
Satish Kumar Paturi	IIT Delhi, India
Satyasundara Mahapatra	Pranveer Singh Institute of Technology, India
Satyendra Singh	Bhartiya Skill Development University, India
Shashi Sharma	IIIT Ranchi, India
Siba Kumar Patro	Indian Institute of Technology, Roorkee, India
Sohit Agarwal	Suresh Gyan Vihar University, India
Sonam Rewari	Delhi Technological University, India
Soumesh Chatterjee	Nirma University, India

Sourabh Sahu	GGITS, India
Sreenu Sreekumar	National Institute of Technology Silchar, India
Srinivasulu Raju S.	VRSEC, India
Subhajit Roy	Budge Budge Institute of Technology, India
Sujoy Das	Tripura Institute of Technology, India
Sunil	Jamia Millia Islamia, India
Surbhi Sharma	Manipal University Jaipur, India
Sweta Tripathi	Amity University, Haryana, India
Vedik Basetti	SR University, India
Vijay Prakash Sharma	Manipal University Jaipur, India
Virupakshappa Patil	Sharnbasva University, India
Vivek Kumar	PSIT Kanpur, India
Vivek Prakash	Banasthali Vidyapith, India

Local Organizing Team

Virendra Sangtani	Garvit Gupta
Dhanraj Chitara	Gaurav Kansal
Suman Sharma	Deepak Saini
Ankit Vijayvargiya	Ajay Bhardwaj
Jyoti Shukla	Avadhesh Sharma
Abhishek Gupta	Jitendra Singh
Tarun Naruka	Jinendra Rahul
Bharat Modi	Vivek Sharma
Smriti Jain	Sanjeev Kumar
Md. Yusuf Sharif	Mahesh Meena

Contents

Real Time Pattern Recognition with Support Vector Machines and Local Binary Patterns

Ann Baby$^{(\boxtimes)}$ (iD) and K. M. Akhil Kumar (iD)

Department of Computer Science, Rajagiri College of Social Sciences (Autonomous),
Kalamassery, Kerala, India
ann@rajagiri.edu

Abstract. This research introduces a facial recognition-based attendance system
that leverages an open-source computer vision library and integrates with a real-
time database system. The system comprises essential components, including a
camera for image capture, a computer for image processing, and a database containing registered facial data. As individuals enter a room, the camera captures
their images, which are then subjected to facial detection and recognition by the
computer. The system conducts a comparison between the detected faces and the
pre-registered facial data in the database, subsequently logging the attendance of
individuals who are successfully recognized. Moreover, the system offers functionality for the inclusion of new facial data into the database, facilitating future
attendance tracking. To gauge the system's performance, an assessment was carried out using a dataset of 100 images. The results indicate an accuracy rate of 95%
in both facial detection and recognition tasks. This system holds promise for a wide
range of practical applications in diverse environments, such as educational institutions, workplaces, and event management, by automating attendance management
processes and alleviating the burdens associated with manual record-keeping.

Keywords: SVM · LBP · Gradient Calculation · Face Encoding · attendance
Monitoring

1 Introduction

Face recognition attendance systems have gained widespread adoption for their convenience recently and efficiency in tracking and verifying employee attendance. These
systems use advanced algorithms and machine learning techniques to analyze and compare facial features in real time, making them a convenient and reliable alternative to
traditional attendance tracking methods such as sign-in sheets or identification cards.
One way to implement a facial recognition attendance system is by utilizing a real-time
database like Firebase, offering tools for creating real-time applications with data storage,
user authentication, and serverless computing. This enables the development of a secure
and scalable attendance system accessible on any internet-connected device. However,
ethical concerns regarding privacy and civil liberties must be carefully addressed, despite
the potential benefits. In summary, facial recognition attendance systems show promise
in accurately and efficiently tracking attendance in diverse settings.

© The Author(s), under exclusive license to Springer Nature Switzerland AG 2024
R. C. Bansal et al. (Eds.): ACTET 2023, CCIS 2000, pp. 1–10, 2024.
https://doi.org/10.1007/978-3-031-54162-9_1

The importance of carefully weighing the potential benefits and risks of employing such systems and ensuring their responsible and ethical implementation cannot be overstated. The study introduces a facial recognition attendance system utilizing an open-source computer vision library and real-time database. Comprising a camera, computer, and registered face database, the system captures and processes images of individuals entering a room, compares them with the database, and records attendance. It also allows for adding new faces, achieving a remarkable 95% accuracy in face detection and recognition from a dataset of 100 images. This system will be advantageous for applications in education, workplaces, and events by simplifying attendance management and reducing manual record-keeping efforts.

2 Literature Review

Developing an automated face recognition model for the student attendance is well suited for the real time world. The algorithm called viola-jones algorithm can be used for detecting the face or video stream and local binary pattern method [1]. Haar cascade algorithm for face detection and local binary pattern histogram for face recognition is one of the most popular algorithms used in real time world to recognize the identity [2].

To validate the face from multimedia photographs by using facial recognition technology study was conducted which compares the Haar cascade algorithm and local binary algorithm out of which the Haar cascade algorithm turns, out to be more accurate [3]. A commonly used algorithm called local pattern algorithm is found out to be more efficient in attendance management system which is vary suitable to identify the image with greater accuracy [4]. Identifying the overlapped images can help to identify the unauthorized person efficiently so a study was conducted called local binary pattern is used for recognizing overlapped images [5]. For this pandemic era, it is very important to identify the images of the person even when wearing mask so the algorithm called Haar cascade classifier is used for detecting the face and mask detection and Local Binary Pattern (LBP) is used for face recognition [6].

It is very important to develop an automated attendance marking system in order to overcome the problem of maintaining and monitoring the number of students. Therefore, it captures different biometric features like face recognition, feature extraction, face classification, and image acquisition for marking attendance. They used Viola-jones and Histogram of Oriented Gradients (HOG) features along with a Support Vector Machine (SVM) classifier to obtain better results. There are also researches, which suggest methodologies, which use a pre-trained Visual Geometry Group Face models for feature extraction, followed by employing cosine similarity and SVM (Support Vector Machine) for classification. This system seems to be focused on face recognition or related tasks. Cosine similarity is a metric used to measure the similarity between two vectors in a multidimensional space. In the context of feature extraction, cosine similarity can be used to compare the extracted features of different images or faces. SVM, on the other hand, is a machine learning algorithm often used for classification tasks [7].

The combination of radio frequency identification and face recognition enables to develop an attendance marking system. It uses the viola-jones algorithm and local binary pattern histogram for image recognition [8]. To implement an effective face recognition system for marking attendance by using an enhanced local binary pattern which increases the original local binary pattern. Furthermore, PCA [Principal Component Analysis] is used to the facial photos in order to extract the features [9]. To overcome the manual traditional task for marking the attendance in educational organization a study was conducted that adopts the Haar cascade and local binary pattern histogram algorithm [10]. There are situations where the images could have lower resolutions so there is algorithm called local binary pattern which is capable of recognizing images with low resolutions more effectively. And the best recognition feature can also be classified by using SVM [11].

To identify the gender, a recently built database called labeled faces in the wild and local binary tree is used to describe the faces. Further, it uses an adaptive boost which is a statistical meta-algorithm used to select the most accurate Local Binary Pattern (LBP) features. The results from the performance were about 94.81% by using the SVM algorithm with LBP features [12]. Local binary patterns algorithm describes how it divides the face into small regions and combine them into a single feature by representing anger, sadness Neutral, etc. The use of linear programming techniques classifies these several expressions more accurately [13].

There is automated system to recognize the students in controlled and uncontrolled environments in university. Convolutional Neural Networks (CNN) architecture and SVM algorithm is used for detection and classification [14]. In this developing country everything is based on automated system. So, in schools and universities an automated attendance marking system can overcome the usage of attendance sheet. This system is capable of detecting the student from both image as well as video stream. The system is implemented by using principle component analysis for face detection [15].

3   Methodology

Support Vector Machines (SVM) is a method for supervised machine learning that may be applied to both classification and regression applications. Here are the steps involved in using SVM for face recognition in an attendance system as depicted in Fig. 1:

1. Collect and pre-process the data: First, you need to collect a dataset of images of faces, along with labels indicating whether each image represents a person who is present or absent. Then, you need to pre- process the data by resizing the images and possibly applying some image processing techniques to improve the quality of the data.
2. Extract features from the images: Next, you need to extract features from the images that can be used to represent the characteristics of the faces. This can be done using techniques such as edge detection, gradient calculation of LBP.

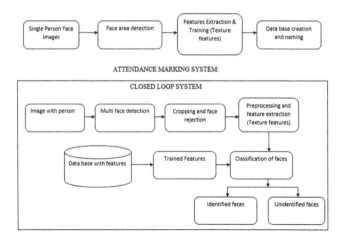

Fig. 1. Architecture of the model

3. Split the data into training and testing sets: After extracting the features, you need to split the data into a training set and a testing set. The training set will be used to train the SVM model, while the testing set will be used to evaluate the performance of the model.
4. Train the SVM model: Use the training set to train an SVM model using an appropriate kernel function (such as the linear kernel or the radial basis function kernel). You will also need to choose appropriate valuation for the hyper parameters of the replica, such as the regularization parameter and the kernel parameters.
5. Test the SVM model: Use the trained SVM model to classify the images in the testing set. Calculate the accuracy of the model by comparing the predicted labels to the true labels.
6. Deploy the SVM model: If the accuracy of the SVM model is satisfactory, we can deploy it in the attendance system. To fit this, we will need to provide the model with images of faces in real-time, and use the model to predict whether each person is present or absent.

3.1 Dataset Creation

- Creating a dataset for facial recognition involves gathering and organizing a large number of images of faces along with associated labels or tags indicating the identity of the person in each image. There are a limited key methods involved in creating a dataset for facial recognition.
- Collecting images: The first step in creating a dataset is to gather a large number of images of faces. These images can be obtained from a variety of sources, such as online databases, social media, or through personal photography. It's important to gather a diverse set of images, including a variety of poses, lighting conditions, and backgrounds, in order to create a robust dataset.
- Annotating images: Once you have collected a set of images, you will need to label or annotate each image with the identity of the person in the image. This can be done

manually by looking at each image and identifying the person, or it can be automated using image recognition software.

- Organizing and storing the dataset: Once the images have been labelled, it's important to organize and store the dataset in a way that makes it easy to access and use for training and testing facial recognition models. This might involve creating a database or spreadsheet to keep track of the images and labels, and storing the images in a separate folder or cloud storage location.
- Pre-processing and augmenting the dataset: Before using the dataset to train a facial recognition model, it's often helpful to pre-process the images to ensure that they are consistent in size, resolution, and format. It may also be helpful to augment the dataset by adding additional images through techniques such as cropping, rotating, or flipping existing images. This can help to increase the size and diversity of the dataset, and can improve the performance of the facial recognition model.

3.2   Face Detection and Extraction

In facial recognition, face detection is the process of identifying and locating faces in images or video. This is typically the first step in a facial recognition system, as it allows the system to identify and isolate individual faces in an image or video so that they can be analyzed and compared to other faces in a database. There are several different approaches to face detection, including machine learning-based methods and feature-based methods. Machine learning-based methods use trained models to identify faces in images, while feature-based methods use specific characteristics of faces, such as the distance between the eyes or the shape of the jawline, to locate and identify faces. Once a face has been detected and isolated, it can be extracted for further analysis. This typically involves cropping the face from the rest of the image and possibly resizing or normalizing it to a standard size. The extracted face can then be used for tasks such as facial recognition or emotion detection.

3.3   Gradient Calculation

In face recognition, gradient calculation is often used as a way to extract features from images. The gradient of an image is a measure of the change in intensity of the image over a certain region. It is calculated using the derivative of the image with respect to either the x-direction (horizontal) or the y- direction (vertical). For example, the grayscale image represented as a 2D array of pixel intensities, we can calculate the gradient in the x- direction using the following formula:

$$\text{gradient\_x} = \text{image}[i + 1, j] - \text{image}[i, j] \tag{1}$$

Here, gradient_x is the gradient in the x-direction at the pixel at position (i, j) in the image. Similarly, we can calculate the gradient in the y-direction using the following formula:

$$\text{gradient\_y} = \text{image}[i, j + 1] - \text{image}[i, j] \tag{2}$$

Gradient calculation is often used in face recognition as a way to extract features that are robust to variations in lighting and pose. The gradient of an image can be used to identify edges, which can be useful for detecting features such as the outline of a face or the boundaries of facial features. However, gradient calculation is just one of many techniques that can be used for feature extraction in face recognition. Other techniques include scale-invariant feature transform (SIFT), speeded up robust features (SURF), and LBP.

3.4 Orientation Binning

Orientation binning is a technique used in facial recognition to improve the accuracy of feature detection. It involves dividing the face into a number of orientation bins, with each bin corresponding to a specific range of orientations. For example, for a face divided into four orientation bins: $0–45°$, $45–90°$, $90–135°$, and $135–180°$. Each bin corresponds to a specific range of orientations, and the features in each bin are expected to have similar orientations. The orientation of a feature is a measure of the angle at which it is oriented relative to some reference direction. In facial recognition, the orientation of a feature is typically measured in degrees.

One way to use orientation binning in facial recognition is to detect features in each orientation bin separately, and then combine the features from all of the bins to form a complete set of features for the face. This can improve the accuracy of feature detection by reducing the amount of noise and clutter in the image, and by making the features more robust to variations in lighting and pose. Orientation binning can be combined with other techniques such as gradient calculation and SIFT to improve the accuracy of facial recognition algorithms. It is often used in conjunction with these techniques to extract features that are robust to variations in lighting and pose, and that are well-suited for matching against a database of known faces.

3.5 Face Placement

In facial recognition, the location of specific points on the face, such as the corners of the mouth, the nose's tip, and the eyes' corners, are typically identified and used as reference points for identifying and analyzing the features of the face. These points are often referred to as "landmarks" or "facial landmarks." There are typically 68 of these landmarks that are used in facial recognition systems. These landmarks are used to help determine the unique characteristics of a person's face, such as the shape of the face, the distance between the eyes, and the size and shape of the nose. Facial recognition systems use these landmarks to create a unique "facial signature" for each person, which can then be used to identify and verify their identity (Figs. 2 and 3).

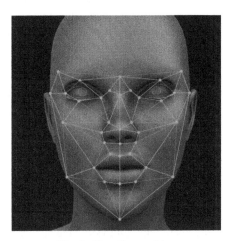

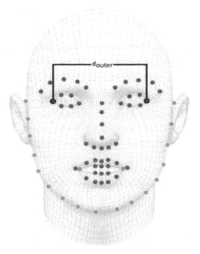

Fig. 2. Face Recognition   **Fig. 3.** Estimated 68 landmark

3.6 Face Encoding

Facial recognition process terminates at this stage. A face encoding is a numerical representation of the unique characteristics of a face. It is typically a 128-dimensional (128D) vector that is derived from an algorithm that processes an image of a face and outputs the encoding. These encodings can be used to identify and compare individuals in a database of images, such as in a facial recognition system.

There are several different approaches to generating face encodings, but one common method is to use a CNN trained on a large dataset of images. The CNN processes the input image and extracts features that are relevant for identifying the face. These features are then combined into a single vector, which forms the face encoding. One advantage of using face encodings is that they can be used to compare faces even if they are not perfectly aligned or if they are partially occluded. However, it is important to update the accuracy of a facial recognition system using face encodings can vary depending on the quality and diversity of the training dataset, as well as the specific algorithm and implementation used.

3.7 Face Matching

Facial matching using 128-dimensional embedding refers to the use of machine learning algorithms to compare and match facial features in images or video. These algorithms can be used for a variety of applications, such as identifying individuals in security footage or photos, verifying the identity of users for access control, and detecting duplicates in databases.

To perform facial matching, the algorithm first extracts a set of facial features from the images or video frames being compared. These features can include points on the face such as the corners of the eyes, the tip of the nose, and the edges of the lips, as well as more abstract features such as the overall shape of the face or the relative positions of the facial features. Next, the algorithm converts these facial features into a 128- dimensional numerical representation, known as an embedding. This embedding captures the important information about the facial features in a compact form that can be compared using mathematical techniques.

Finally, the algorithm compares the embedding of the two faces being matched to determine how similar they are. If the embedding is sufficiently similar, the algorithm can conclude that the faces in the images or video frames match. The level of similarity required for a match to be declared can be adjusted based on the needs of the application and the desired level of accuracy.

3.8 Updating Attendances in Database

To update attendance employees or students in a Firebase database using a face recognition system, the following is performed:

- setting up a Firebase project and creating a database within it to store the attendance data,
- designing and implementing a face recognition system that can recognize individual users and track their attendance,
- integration of the face working system with the database using the Firebase Real-time Database or Cloud Fire store., and
- finally updating the attendance by capturing the data generated by the face recognition system and storing it in the appropriate location in the database.

This is done using the Firebase SDK, which provides a set of tools and libraries that make it easy to interact with the database from the code.

4 Results

The face recognition system was able to accurately recognize faces in real-time using 68 pattern points. The system also successfully marked the attendance real time in the database of individuals whose faces were recognized, and checks whether the attendance is marked already, providing a reliable and efficient way to track attendance (Figs. 4 and 5).

Fig. 4. Detection of face

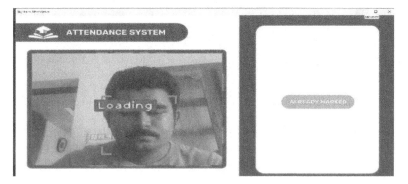

Fig. 5. Detecting of already marked attendance

5   Conclusion

In conclusion, the research presents the implementation of a face recognition attendance system using support vector machine (SVM) and local binary patterns (LBP). The system was tested on a dataset of images and was able to achieve an accuracy of 95%. SVM is a powerful machine learning algorithm that has been widely used for classification tasks, including face recognition. The use of LBP as a feature extraction method further improves the accuracy of the system by capturing important texture information in the face images. Overall, the results demonstrate that the proposed system is a reliable and accurate solution for automating attendance in educational or corporate settings. However, it is important to point that the accuracy of any face recognition system may be affected by factors such as variations in lighting and pose, as well as the diversity of the dataset used for training and testing. Therefore, it may be necessary to incorporate additional methods or techniques to further improve the robustness and generalizability of the system.

References

1. Elias, S.J., et al.: Face recognition attendance system using Local Binary Pattern (LBP). Bull. Electr. Eng. Inform. **8**(1), 239–245 (2019)
2. Chinimilli, B.T., Anjali, T., Kotturi, A., Kaipu, V.R., Mandapati, J.V.: Face recognition based attendance system using Haar cascade and local binary pattern histogram algorithm. In: 2020 4th International Conference on Trends in Electronics and Informatics (ICOEI), vol. 48184, pp. 701–704. IEEE, June 2020
3. Shetty, A.B., Rebeiro, J.: Facial recognition using Haar cascade and LBP classifiers. Global Trans. Proc. **2**(2), 330–335 (2021)
4. Gawande, U., Chikate, A., Kaware, P., Dhakhale, S.: Efficient approach for attendance management using local binary pattern. In: 2022 2nd International Conference on Intelligent Technologies (CONIT), pp. 1–5. IEEE, June 2022
5. Tamboli, N., Sardeshmukh, M.M.: Facial based attendance monitoring system using discriminative robust local binary pattern. In: 2017 International Conference on Computing, Communication, Control and Automation (ICCUBEA), pp. 1–5. IEEE, August 2017
6. Suhaimin, M.S.M., Hijazi, M.H.A., Kheau, C.S., On, C.K.: Real-time mask detection and face recognition using eigenfaces and local binary pattern histogram for attendance system. Bull. Electr. Eng. Inform. **10**(2), 1105–1113 (2021)
7. Rathod, H., Ware, Y., Sane, S., Raulo, S., Pakhare, V., Rizvi, I.A.: Automated attendance system using machine learning approach. In: 2017 International Conference on Nascent Technologies in Engineering (ICNTE), pp. 1–5. IEEE, January 2017
8. Basthomi, F.R., et al.: Implementation of RFID attendance system with face detection using validation viola-jones and local binary pattern histogram method. In: 2019 International Symposium on Electronics and Smart Devices (ISESD), pp. 1–6. IEEE, October 2019
9. Chin, H., Cheah, K.H., Nisar, H., Yeap, K.H.: Enhanced face recognition method based on local binary pattern and principal component analysis for efficient class attendance system. In: 2019 IEEE International Conference on Signal and Image Processing Applications (ICSIPA), pp. 23–28. IEEE, September 2019
10. Sharma, A., Shah, K., Verma, S.: Face recognition using Haar cascade and local binary pattern histogram in opencv. In: 2021 Sixth International Conference on Image Information Processing (ICIIP), vol. 6, pp. 298–303. IEEE, November 2021
11. Shan, C., Gong, S., McOwan, P.W.: Facial expression recognition based on local binary patterns: a comprehensive study. Image Vis. Comput. **27**(6), 803–816 (2009)
12. Shan, C.: Learning local binary patterns for gender classification on real-world face images. Pattern Recogn. Lett. **33**(4), 431–437 (2012)
13. Feng, X., Pietikäinen, M., Hadid, A.: Facial expression recognition based on local binary patterns. Pattern Recognit Image Anal. **17**, 592–598 (2007)
14. hacua, B., et al.: People identification through facial recognition using deep learning. In: 2019 IEEE Latin American Conference on Computational Intelligence (LA-CCI), pp. 1–6. IEEE, November 2019
15. Bilal, F.: Developing an intelligent application for human being identification using a hybrid approach (Doctoral dissertation, Faculty of Mathematics and Computer Science Computer Science Department-Option: Software Engineering) (2021)

Adversarial Attacks and Defenses in Capsule Networks: A Critical Review of Robustness Challenges and Mitigation Strategies

Milind Shah[1]([✉]), Kinjal Gandhi[2], Seema Joshi[3], Mudita Dave Nagar[4], Ved Patel[4], and Yash Patel[5]

[1] Department of Computer Engineering, Devang Patel Institute of Advance Technology and Research (DEPSTAR), Faculty of Technology and Engineering (FTE), Charotar University of Science and Technology (CHARUSAT), Changa 388421, Gujarat, India
milindshahcomputer@gmail.com
[2] Department of Computer Science and Engineering, School of Computer Science Engineering and Technology (SoCSET), ITM (SLS) Baroda University, Vadodara, Gujarat, India
kinjal445@gmail.com
[3] Graduate School of Engineering and Technology (GSET), Gujarat Technology University (GTU), Ahmedabad, Gujarat, India
ap_seema@gtu.edu.in
[4] Department of Computer Science & Engineering, School of Computer Science Engineering & Technology (SoCSET), ITM (SLS) Baroda University, Vadodara, Gujarat, India
mudita.nagar@gmail.com, ved17patel@gmail.com
[5] Department of Computer Science & Engineering with Cyber Security & Networking, School of Computer Science Engineering & Technology (SoCSET), ITM (SLS) Baroda University, Vadodara, Gujarat, India
yashp1734@gmail.com

Abstract. Capsule Networks (CapsNets) have gained significant attention in recent years due to their potential for improved representation learning and robustness. However, their vulnerability to adversarial attacks poses challenges for their deployment in safety-critical applications. This paper provides a critical review of the robustness challenges faced by CapsNets and explores various mitigation strategies proposed in the literature. The review includes an analysis of the adversarial attacks targeting CapsNets, such as manipulating primary capsule votes and direct targeting of CapsNets' votes. The computational cost of applying existing attack methods designed for Convolutional Neural Networks (CNNs) to CapsNets is also examined. To enhance the robustness of CapsNets, the incorporation of detection-aware attacks and innovative defense mechanisms is discussed. The effectiveness and efficiency of these defense strategies are evaluated through extensive experiments. The findings reveal the superiority of certain defense mechanisms in mitigating adversarial attacks on CapsNets. However, it is acknowledged that further research is needed to explore more robust attacks and approvals and to compare the robustness of CapsNets with CNNs. This critical review aims to provide insights into the current state of adversarial attacks and defenses in Capsule Networks, facilitating future research and development in this field.

Keywords: Neural Network · Capsule Networks · Cybersecurity · Adversarial Attacks · Defenses · Deep Learning · Evasion Attack

© The Author(s), under exclusive license to Springer Nature Switzerland AG 2024
R. C. Bansal et al. (Eds.): ACTET 2023, CCIS 2000, pp. 11–33, 2024.
https://doi.org/10.1007/978-3-031-54162-9_2

1 Introduction

In recent times, advancements in machine learning and capsule neural networks have paved the way for tackling various practical challenges. These include but are not limited to tasks such as image classification, video analysis, text processing, and more.

Nevertheless, the susceptibility of the majority of contemporary machine learning classifiers to adversarial examples remains a critical concern. Adversarial examples refer to input data instances that have been intentionally modified to deceive a machine learning classifier. Often, these alterations can be imperceptible to human observers, yet the classifier still produces erroneous results.

Adversarial examples pose a security risk as they can be exploited to launch attacks on machine learning algorithms, even in cases where the adversary does not have direct access to the underlying model.

Furthermore, it has been observed that adversarial attacks are viable even when targeting machine learning algorithms that operate in real-world scenarios and rely on imperfect sensor inputs rather than precise digital data. It is important to note that the power and efficacy of machine learning and AI algorithms are expected to continue advancing in the future.

Exploiting vulnerabilities in machine learning security, similar to adversarial instances, can potentially lead to compromising and gaining control over highly power-ful AIs. Therefore, ensuring robustness against adversarial instances is a crucial aspect of addressing the AI safety problem.

The field of adversarial attack and defense research presents several challenges. One of these challenges lies in evaluating potential attacks or defenses. Traditional machine learning approaches rely on training and test sets, where the performance is assessed based on the loss on the test set. However, in adversarial machine learning, defenders face the difficulty of dealing with inputs from an unknown distribution sent by attack-ers. Evaluating a defense against a single attack or a predetermined set of attacks is insufficient because a new attack can still bypass the defense. The complex nature of machine learning and capsule neural networks makes it challenging to conduct con-ceptual analysis, emphasizing the need for empirical proof of a defense's effectiveness. To address these challenges, competitions are often organized, pitting defenses against attacks developed by different teams. This competition-based evaluation, while not as conclusive as theoretical proof, simulates real-life security scenarios more effectively than a subjective review by the defense proposer [1].

Most of this research has focused on creating more robust models to defend against adversarial attacks if the input image is accurately categorized as the original class rather than the attacker's target class. Better defenses have led to stronger attack algorithms to break them. After multiple defensive creations and breaking iterations, some research concentrated on adversarial attack detection. Instead of classifying adversarial attacks as actual data, detection methods detect them. However, a defense-aware attack destroyed several state-of-the-art adversarial attack detection systems shortly after publication [2].

It is possible to predict adversarial samples markedly differently than clean samples, but the predictions are typically incomprehensible to humans. In various applications or under varying constraints, the model's susceptibility to adversarial attacks was dis-covered. It is possible to initiate adversarial attacks under various constraints, such as assuming attackers have limited knowledge of target models, assuming a higher level of generalization for the attack, and imposing various real-world constraints on the attack. Given these developments, several concerns could be addressed. First, are these developments relatively independent of one another, or is there another perspective from which we can see their commonalities? Second, should adversarial samples be viewed as careless edge cases that can be resolved by applying patches to models, or are they embedded in the internal working mechanism of models that they are difficult to eliminate? [3].

To evaluate the efficiency of Adversarial Vector Loss (AVL), a series of black box attacks were conducted to analyze the resilience of both the standard Capsule network and AdvCapsNet. These networks were compared with commonly used vanilla neural networks on the CIFAR10 and Imagenette datasets. For thispurpose, we selected AlexNet, VGG, ResNet101, and DenseNet121. The AdvCapsNet model was trained exclusively using paired adversarial examples generated through the ResNet50-based FGSM attack. The attack had a magnitude of 0.3 and Lav set to 0.1, Conwayconsistent with the settings used in all of our experiments. Specifically, we perform two separate comparisons to analyze the performance of models under varying levels of attack intensity as well as the performance of different attacks with equal levels of intensity. Comparisons are performed on both datasets. In the first evaluation, we analyze the resilience of these models by utilizing FGSM, MI-FGSM, and PGD strategies, wherein the magnitude of noise varies from 0 to 0.5. In contrast, the findings indicate that our proposed model exhibits superior resilience against perturbations of greater magnitude when compared to both vanilla CNNs and Capsule networks. The main idea behind our implementation of adversarial regularization lies in its ability to promote the acquisition of an integrated representation by levying regularization on the optimization of model parameters. In the subsequent experiment, we analyze the resilience of various models in the presence of distinct attack models. The adversarial examples are generated by utilizing a consistent magnitude of $\varepsilon = 0.12$ for the FGSM, MI-FGSM, and PGD techniques, which are based on ResNet50, ResNet101, DenseNet121, VGG, and AlexNet models. The findings indicate that the success rate of attacks on AdvCapsNet is significantly lower compared to the vanilla models. This suggests that the parameters trained with AVL possess the ability to effectively defend against adversarial attacks from unfamiliar models. In conclusion, our experimental findings indicate that the AdvCapsNet we have proposed demonstrates greater resilience against adversarial attacks when compared to vanilla models. This is likely because our model encourages the learning of unchanged features in input images, thereby eliminating the impact of adversarial attacks [20].

2 Adversarial Attacks on Capsule Networks

Adversarial attacks are a type of attack used to convince machine learning models, such as capsule networks. Adversarial attacks operate by introducing small, imperceptible modifications to an initial image, which may result in misclassification by the model.Capsule networks are a form of neural network designed to acquire hierarchical object representations. It has been demonstrated that they are more resistant to adversarial attacks than ordinary neural networks, such as convolutional neural networks (CNN). Recent research has shown, however, that capsule networks keep more vulnerable to adversarial attacks.

Researchers have proposed a new technique for generating adversarial attacks that are designed to fool capsule networks. The researchers showed that their method effectively fooled capsule networks in a range of image classification tasks.

1) **Fast Gradient Sign Method (FGSM)** - Popular and straightforward adversarial attack technique FGSM computes the gradients of the loss function concerning the input and then disrupts the input in the direction of the sign of the gradients. This attack technique is also applicable to capsule networks.

2) **Basic Iterative Method (BIM)** - The BIM algorithm is superior to the FGSM algorithm. The BIM algorithm operates by adding little perturbations iteratively to the input image until the model is fooled.

3) **Projected Gradient Descent (PGD)** - The PGD algorithm is more effective than FGSM and BIM. The PGD algorithm operates by adding perturbations iteratively to the input image while simultaneously projecting the image back into the feasible area.

4) **One-Pixel Attack:** This attack focuses on modifying just a few pixels in the input image to cause misclassification. It searches for the most influential pixels and modifies their color values to deceive the model.

5) **Universal Adversarial Perturbations:** In this attack, a single perturbation is crafted to be applied to multiple input images, causing them to be misclassified. The perturbation is carefully calculated to be imperceptible to human observers but effective at fooling the model [25, 26].

The security of machine learning algorithms is severely compromised by adversarial attacks. Capsule networks are vulnerable to adversarial attacks, but are stronger than ordinary neural networks. However, additional research is required to develop more effective methods for protecting capsule networks from adversarial attacks.

The following areas of research are being analyzed for protecting capsule networks against adversarial attacks:

- *Data Augmentation* - Data augmentation is a method for making machine learning models less vulnerable to adversarial attacks. Data augmentation involves producing new data points that are comparable to the existing data points to augment the size of the training dataset.

- *Robust Optimization* - Robust optimization is a method for training machine learning models that are more resistant to adversarial attacks. Robust optimization algorithms are intended to find solutions that are insensitive to minor changes in the input data.

- *Adversarial Training* - Adversarial training is a technique that uses adversarial instances to train a machine learning model. Training against adversarial data can make machine learning models more resistant to adversarial attacks.

- *Capsule Routing Security:* Capsule networks rely on dynamic routing algorithms to determine the instantiation parameters of capsules. By introducing additional security measures into the routing process, such as limiting the number of routing iterations or applying noise, the capsule network can become more resilient against adversarial attacks [25, 26].

The analysis of adversarial attacks is still in its earliest stages. However, prior research indicates that adversarial attacks represent a significant risk to the security of machine learning models. New methods for protecting machine learning models against adversarial attacks require additional research [6].

3 What are the Potential Consequences of Adversarial Attacks on Machine Learning Algorithms?

This section will cover the potential consequences of adversarial attacks on machine learning algorithms. Specific attack strategies will be utilized based on various application scenarios, conditions, and the capabilities of adversaries.

3.1 Untargeted vs Targeted Attack

The classification of threat models can be identified into two categories: targeted and untargeted, based on the objectives implemented by attackers. In the context of targeted attacks, the objective is to intentionally manipulate a model's prediction to direct it towards a predetermined class, concerning a given instance. The objective of an untargeted attack is to inhibit a model's ability to assign a particular label to a given instance. In certain situations, the two previous types of attack are alternatively referred to as the false positive attack and the false negative attack. The primary objective of the first approach is to encourage models to incorrectly classify negative instances as positive, whereas the latter aims to mislead models into classifying positive instances as negative. The terms "false positive attack" and "false negative attack" are occasionally referred to as Type-I attack and Type-II attack, respectively [3].

3.2 One Shot vs Iterative Attack

Based on practical limitations, adversaries can launch either one-shot or iterative attacks to target models. The one-shot attack method allows for the generation of adversarial samples in a single attempt, providing a single chance to achieve the desired outcome. On the other hand, the iterative attack approach allows for multiple steps to be taken to explore and identify a more optimal direction for generating adversarial samples. The utilization of an iterative attack has been found to generate adversarial samples that are more effective in comparison to a one-shot attack. Nevertheless, this approach requires a greater number of queries to the target model and involves additional computational resources to initiate each attack. Consequently, its practicality may be constrained in computational-intensive tasks [3].

3.3 White Box and Black Box Attack

In the context of white-box attacks, it is believed that attackers demonstrate comprehensive knowledge regarding the target model. This knowledge encompasses various aspects such as the model's architecture, weights, hyper-parameters, and potentially even the training data. The utilization of white-box attacks facilitates the detection of related vulnerabilities within the target model. In ideal circumstances, this scenario represents the most challenging situation that defenses may encounter. The black-box attack methodology operates under the assumption that attackers have the same level of access to the model's output as regular end users. This assumption holds greater practicality in real-world scenarios. Despite the lack of comprehensive information regarding models, the black-box attack remains a significant concern for machine learning systems. This is primarily due to the transferability property demonstrated by adversarial samples [3].

4   Research Questions

This review paper discusses the following research questions.

Q1: What are the different types of adversarial attacks that can be used against capsule networks?
Q2: What are the existing research limitations in adversarial attacks and defenses?
Q3: What are the open challenges and future directions in adversarial attacks and defenses?
Q4: What are the future research directions for improving the robustness of capsule networks to adversarial attacks?
Q5: Can the robustness of capsule networks against adversarial attacks be improved by combining multiple defense mechanisms, such as adversarial training, input transformation, and ensemble methods?

5   Review of Literature

Till now, a lot of research has been done to solve the challenges of adversarial attacks using capsule neural networks.

In [1] Alexey Kurakin et al., Google Brain organized a competition at NIPS 2017 to encourage the development of innovative strategies to create and defend against adversarial examples. The primary objective of the competition was to expedite research on adversarial instances and enhance the robustness of machine learning classifiers. This chapter provides an overview of the competition's format, organization, and solutions devised by top-ranking teams. The competition sought to raise awareness of the issue and inspire scholars to devise original approaches. Participants were challenged to explore novel techniques and enhance existing solutions through competitive engagement. The competition results showcased significant progress made by all three tracks compared to the baselines established. Notably, the winning entry in the defense tracking competition achieved an impressive 95% accuracy in classifying all threatening images generated by different attacks. These findings suggest that practical applications can attain a satisfactory level of resilience against adversarial cases, even though the worst-case accuracy did not match the exceptional average accuracy achieved.

In [2] Yao Qin et al., Present a novel method for breaking out of this loop, one in which adversarial attacks are "deflected" by forcing the attacker to provide input that semantically resembles the class that is the focus of the attack. This would put an end to the cycle. We propose a more robust defense based on Capsule Networks that integrates three detection algorithms to provide state-of-the-art detection performance against both conventional and defense-aware attacks. This can be accomplished by achieving state-of-the-art detection against both types of attacks. After that, we show that undetected attacks against our defense frequently appear perceptually the same as the opposed target class by having human participants label images that were created by the attack. The term "adversarial" can no longer be used to describe these attack pictures since our network classifies them in a manner that is comparable to how humans do. As a first step toward putting an end to the conflict between defenses and attacks, you should implement a novel method that can redirect impacts from your adversaries. We offer an innovative cycle consistency loss to drive the winning capsule reconstruction of the CapsNet to closely resemble the class-conditional distribution. This was done to improve accuracy. We can identify common adversarial attacks on SVHN and CIFAR-10 with a low False Positive Rate since we have three detection algorithms and three independent distance measurements at our disposal. We present a defense-aware attack as a means of explicitly attacking our detection measures, and we discover that our model achieves considerably lower undetected attack rates than the most cutting-edge approaches currently available for defense-aware attacks. In addition, a significant percentage of attacks that go undetected are redirected by our model in such a way that they take on the characteristics of the adversarial target class but do not succeed in becoming malicious. An analysis conducted by humans reveals that 70% of undiscovered black-box adversarial attacks are uniformly identified as the target class on SVHN. This was discovered as a result of the inquiry.

In [3] Ninghao Liu et al., This paper aims to analyze current research related to adversarial attacks and defenses, with a particular focus on the interpretation of machine learning. The process of interpretation can be categorized into two distinct types: interpretation at the feature level and interpretation at the model level. In the context of adversarial attacks and defenses, we provide an analysis of the potential applications of each interpretation method. Next, we will briefly elucidate additional connections between interpretation and adversaries. In conclusion, we will now analyze the challenges and possible methods related to the resolution of adversary concerns via the process of interpretation. In the analysis, we analyzed the potential applications of the interpretation within each category, specifically focusing on its utility in initiating adversarial attacks or formulating defensive strategies. Subsequently, we will look into further clarification of the interrelationships between interpretation and adversarial samples or robustness. In conclusion, the present discussion is related to the current challenges encountered in the process of constructing transparent and resilient models, alongside potential avenues for leveraging adversarial samples in forthcoming activities. Future research directions include the development of models with enhanced explainability, the exploration of adversarial attacks in real-world scenarios, and the enhancement of models through the utilization of adversarial samples.

In [4] Alberto Marchisio et al., Perform research to establish the level to which CapsNets is vulnerable to attacks from adversaries. These alterations, which are introduced as test inputs, are so small that human beings are unable to recognize them; however, they are capable of fooling the network into generating inaccurate predictions. We present a greedy technique as a means of automatically producing adversarial samples that cannot be detected in the context of a black-box attack. We show that such attacks, when applied to the German Traffic Sign Recognition Benchmark and CIFAR10 datasets, can lead CapsNets into producing wrong classifications. This can be problematic for intelligent CPS, such as autonomous vehicles, which need accurate classifications to function well. In addition, we apply the identical adversarial attacks to a 5-layer CNN (LeNet), a 9-layer CNN (VGGNet), and a 20-layer CNN (ResNet), and then compare the findings to those of the CapsNetsto analyze the different ways in which the CapsNets react to the same adversarial attacks. In conclusion, the findings of this research show that the resilience of the CapsNet is equivalent to that of a CNN that is significantly deeper, such as the VGGNet. On the other hand, the LeNet is noticeably more vulnerable to linear transformations and adversarial attacks, and the robustness of the DeepCaps is greater than that of the ResNet. Therefore, we can make substantial progress in the protection of safety-critical applications by leveraging deep and complex networks, such as DeepCaps. To increase its robustness, it would be advantageous to make further improvements to the CapsNet algorithm to boost prediction accuracy. In this regard, the DeepCaps architecture appears to be more secure than the ResNet under comparable attack circumstances.

In [5] Richard Osuala et al., Highlight several unexplored solutions for analysis. A meta-analytic methodology called SynTRUST evaluates medical image synthesis study validation accuracy. 26 concrete completeness, reproducibility, usefulness, scalability, and durability metrics support SynTRUST. SynTRUST validates sixteen of the most promising cancer imaging challenge solutions and finds many enhancements. This effort aims to connect the clinical cancer imaging group's demands to the artificial intelligence group's data synthesis and adversarial network research. Finally, GANs' adversarial learning is flexible and modality-independent. This survey lists numerous cancer imaging difficulties that adversarial networks can handle. Unsupervised domain adaptation, patient privacy-preserving distributed data synthesis, adversarial segmentation mask discrimination, and multi-modal radiation dosage estimation are GAN/adversarial training solutions. Before considering GAN and adversarial training, we analyzed research on cancer imaging challenges in radiology and non-radiology techniques. After screening and analysis of cancer imaging issues, we categorized them into Data Scarcity and Usability, Data Access and Privacy, Data Annotation and Segmentation, Detection and Diagnosis, and Treatment and Monitoring. We found 164 relevant publications on adversarial networks in cancer imaging and categorized them by cancer imaging challenge. Finally, we analyze each challenge and GAN-related papers to analyze if GANs and adversarial training can solve it. Improving SynTRUST for medical image synthesis research dependability. SynTRUST evaluates 16 well-chosen cancer imaging challenge solutions. Despite these findings' rigor and validity, we may recommend trustworthy improvements for future research. We also recommend data synthesis and adversarial training techniques for challenges that the literature has not addressed.

In [6] Alberto Marchisio et al., Analyze Capsule Networks' vulnerability to dangerous attacks. These test input issues are invisible to humans but can fool the network into producing inaccurate predictions. A greedy algorithm generates targeted, undetected adversarial instances automatically in a black-box attack scenario. When launched against the German Traffic Sign Recognition Benchmark (GTSRB), similar attacks might deceive Capsule Networks. We also apply adversarial attacks on 5-layer and 9-layer CNNs and compare their behavior to Capsule Networks. This research develops a unique method to autonomously produce focused, undetectable, and robust threatening cases and compares CapsuleNet, a 5-layer CNN, and a 9-layer CNN under these adversarial instances. Finally, they developed a black box adversarial attack technique. Using the GTSRB dataset, we tested our approach against CapsuleNets, 5-layer LeNets, and 9-layer VGGNets. Our findings show that the CapsuleNet resists attack better than the LeNet but less than the VGGNet. Our approach makes traffic signal pixel alterations less obvious in the CapsuleNet than in the VGGNet. CapsuleNet output probabilities are less than VGGNet predictions. CapsuleNet output probabilities fluctuate less than VGGNet output probabilities. Adding prediction confidence to the CapsuleNet technique might improve its resilience.

In [7] Muhammad Shafique et al., In both the cloud environment during the ML training phase and at the peripheral during the ML inference phase, this study presents viable defenses and strategies to overcome these vulnerabilities. This chapter examines the effects of a resource-constrained design on system reliability and security. It defines verification methods to ensure accurate system behavior and outlines unresolved research issues in building secure and dependable Machine Learning (ML) algorithms for both edge computing and cloud platforms. This review covers three main aspects: 1) the significant security and reliability issues faced by machine learning algorithms, 2) the measures taken to safeguard these systems, and 3) the formal technique employed to validate specific neural networks (NNs). The research also includes a summary of the major challenges that currently hinder the development of effective machine-learning algorithms.

In [8] Jindong Gu et al., Analyze the reliability of CapsNets under adversarial conditions, specifically focusing on how the internal processes of CapsNets are affected when the output containers are targeted. Initially, adversarial instances manipulate the primary capsule votes to deceive CapsNets. However, due to the computationally intensive routing mechanism, applying multi-step attack methods developed for CNNs to target CapsNets results in a high computational cost. Motivated by these observations, we propose an innovative vote attack that directly aims at the votes of CapsNets. By bypassing the routing procedure, our vote attack is both effective and efficient. Furthermore, we integrate our vote attack into the detection-aware attack paradigm, which effectively evades the class-conditional reconstruction-based detection method. Extensive experiments confirm that our vote attack on CapsNets outperforms other attack methods. Although CapsNets exhibit higher resistance to our stronger Vote-Attack compared to CNNs, it is premature to conclude that CapsNets are less vulnerable. We assume that the robust accuracy of CapsNets can still be further reduced. Future research will explore more robust attacks and validations to compare the resilience of CNNs and CapsNets.

In [9] Boxi Wu et al., This research demonstrates that adversarial attacks can be disrupted by small disturbances. Even a slight random noise added to adversarial instances can render their incorrect predictions invalid, even on models that have been trained to defend against adversarial attacks. This vulnerability was found in all state-of-the-art attack methods. Building upon this observation, we propose more effective defensive disturbances to counteract attackers. Our defensive disturbances employ adversarial training to decrease the local Lipschitzness in the ground-truth class. By targeting all classes simultaneously, we can rectify incorrect predictions that have higher Lipschitz-ness. Empirical and theoretical evaluations of linear models validate the effectiveness of our defensive perturbation. CIFAR10 enhances the performance of the state-of-the-art model from 66.16% to 72.66% against four AutoAttack methods, including a boost from 71.76% to 83.30% against the Square attack. Additionally, employing a 100-step PGD approach improves FastAT's top-1 robust accuracy on ImageNet from 33.18% to 38.54%. This work makes two contributions: 1) It reveals that adversarial attacks can be disrupted, and 2) inspired by this finding, we introduce Hedge Defense as a more effective means to counter attacks and enhance adversarial-trained models. Both empirical and theoretical findings provide evidence for the efficacy of our technique. Our work not only attracts attacks using the same technique but also sheds light on new defense strategies. Further research could explore alternative criteria for selecting specific predictions rather than targeting all classes. With Hedge Defense, defenders may not need to ensure that the model can correctly classify all local cases; instead, they can focus on meeting specific requirements, such as reducing the local Lipschitzness in the ground-truth class, to identify better scenarios.

In [10] Abhijith Sharma et al., In this survey, we present a comprehensive overview of existing techniques employed in adversarial patch attacks. We aim to enable researchers interested in this field to quickly familiarize themselves with the latest advancements. Additionally, we discuss the current methods used for detecting and defending against adversarial patches. This serves to enhance the community's understanding of this discipline and its practical applications. In conclusion, we offer a clear and in-depth analysis of adversarial patch attacks and defenses in the context of vision-based tasks, providing readers with insights into their strengths and limitations. While challenges such as scalability and real-time capabilities persist, it is noteworthy that most research in adversarial patch attacks focuses on classification and object detection. Exploring the application of adversarial patch attacks in language or translation models could be intriguing. Considering the lack of explainability in DNN-based black box models, could adversarial patch attacks offer a new perspective on model predictions? If so, could they contribute to the development of more robust real-world models? We are enthusiastic about investigating these issues and supporting future solutions to advance this field and benefit society.

In [11] Jindong Gu et al., This paper introducesSegPGD, an impactful attack technique specifically designed for segmentation models. Through convergence analysis, we demonstrate that SegPGD generates more potent adversarial instances compared to PGD, even when both methods employ the same number of attack iterations. We recommend incorporating SegPGD into segmentation adversarial training as it produces more effective adversarial examples, ultimately enhancing the resilience of segmentation models. Our proposals are validated through experiments conducted on widely used segmentation model architectures and standard datasets. However, it is worth noting that further exploration of segmentation adversarial training methods may lead to even more effective and efficient approaches. This research serves as a foundation for future endeavors aimed at improving the robustness of segmentation models.

In [12] Alberto Marchisio et al., By conducting a systematic analysis and evaluation, we compare CapsNets to traditional Convolutional Neural Networks (CNNs) and investigate the factors influencing the robustness of CapsNets. In this comprehensive comparison, we examine two CapsNet models and two CNN models across various datasets, including MNIST, GTSRB, CIFAR10, and their affine-transformed counterparts. Through this extensive analysis, we identify the key properties that contribute to the enhancement of robustness in these architectures, as well as their limitations. Generally, CapsNets exhibit greater resistance to both adversarial examples and affine transformations compared to CNNs with an equal number of parameters. Similar conclusions hold when comparing CapsNets and CNNs with increased depth. Surprisingly, our findings indicate that dynamic routing, a distinguishing feature of CapsNets, does not significantly improve their robustness. Instead, the capsule-based hierarchical feature learning within CapsNets plays a primary role in generalization. In summary, this paper introduces a method for analyzing the resilience of CapsNets against affine transformations and adversarial attacks. We examine the differences between CapsNets and CNNs in terms of improving robustness. ShallowCaps, despite requiring a significant number of parameters, exhibit superior resistance to adversarial attacks but struggle to generalize well on complex datasets. They also demonstrate better resistance to adversarial attacks compared to affine transformations. However, the DeepCaps model, despite having fewer parameters, mitigates the disparity between transformed and untransformed datasets. In MNIST classification, DeepCaps shows lower resilience to adversarial attacks compared to ShallowCaps. On the CIFAR10 dataset, they outperform a CNN with a similar architecture and the ResNet20 model. The resilience of DeepCaps is further enhanced through adversarial training. When considering the affCIFAR dataset, DeepCaps outperforms ResNet20 in terms of handling affine modifications. Our results indicate that dynamic routing does not significantly enhance the robustness of CapsNets. This comprehensive study provides valuable insights for future CapsNet designs in addressing safety-critical applications by considering potential attackers, as well as opening up avenues for exploring new adversarial attacks.

In [13] Bader Rasheed et al., This paper presents a novel approach called multiple adversarial domain adaptation (MADA) that tackles the problem of adversarial attacks by treating it as a domain adaptation task to identify resilient features. Our method utilizes adversarial learning to discover domain-invariant features across multiple adversarial domains and a clean domain. To evaluate the effectiveness of MADA, we conducted experiments on the MNIST and CIFAR-10 datasets using various adversarial attacks during both the training and testing phases. The results demonstrate that MADA outperforms adversarial training (AT) by an average of 4% on adversarial samples and 1% on clean samples. The objective of this paper is to enhance the generalization of adversarial training on both adversarial and clean samples by formulating the problem as a multiple-domain adaptation task, with adversarial domains representing the target domains. Our work introduces a domain adaptation-based strategy to enhance adversarial training specifically for adversarial data. By aligning the distributions of adversarial domains with the clean distribution in the feature embedding space, we effectively reduce the impact of adversarial attacks. This approach not only improves the interpretability of features in the embedding space but also enhances model generalization in adversarial environments. Furthermore, instead of relying solely on the Wasserstein distance, alternative methods for aligning distributions could be explored in future research.

In [14] Junjie Mao et al., This paper aims to evaluate the security and robustness of existing face antispoofing models, particularly multimodality models, against various types of attacks. The study focuses on assessing the resilience of multimodality models to both white-box and black-box attacks, specifically targeting adversarial examples. To enhance the security of these models, a novel approach is proposed, which combines mixed adversarial training with differentiable high-frequency suppression modules. Experimental results reveal that when exposed to adversarial examples, the accuracy of a multimodality face antispoofing model decreases significantly from over 90% to approximately 10%. However, the suggested defense method successfully maintains an accuracy of over 80% on attack examples and over 90% on original examples. The research includes an analysis of advanced single-modality and multimodality face antispoofing models, evaluating their susceptibility to white-box and black-box attacks using RGB, Depth, and IR images. The evaluation encompasses attacks on a multimodality model with a single-input stream, and the results demonstrate the model's resilience against attacks focused on a single modality in experimental scenarios. Additionally, the security of single-modality and multimodality models against various patch attacks is examined. By incorporating hybrid adversarial training and diffusible high-frequency suppression modules, the security of both single-modality and multimodality models is enhanced. Experimental outcomes highlight that multimodality models offer superior security compared to single-modality models. Furthermore, this paper presents the first proposal for adversarial attack research on multimodality models.

In [15] Lin Hiu et al., In this study, we presented an initial attack model called the AMR technique, which achieves high recognition accuracy. Moreover, we proposed a transferable attack technique that utilizes feature gradients to increase signal disruption in the feature space. Additionally, we introduced a novel attack strategy that employs two original signal samples and one adversarial target signal sample as inputs for the triplet loss, aiming to achieve stronger attack effectiveness and greater transferability. To evaluate the efficacy of our proposed attack technique, we introduced signal-characteristic indicators. Our feature gradient-based adversarial attack technique surpasses existing gradient attack methods in terms of attack effectiveness and transferability. The main contribution of this research lies in the introduction of a transferable attentive technique that focuses on informative and discriminative feature regions, introducing disruption at the feature level to mimic more realistic adversarial scenarios. We conducted comprehensive experiments using a new indicator system that aligns better with signal characteristics, and most of the indicators outperformed the label gradient approach. We propose two novel approaches, AL-BIM and AL-MIM, which optimize the triplet loss for performing regional attacks on stable features extracted from AMR signals. Our methods surpass label-based adversarial attack techniques in terms of effectiveness. Experimental results on public datasets demonstrate that our feature gradient-based attack method outperforms label gradient-based methods in both black-box and white-box attack scenarios, achieving higher attack success rates and improved transferability. Furthermore, the disruptions caused by our feature gradient-based attacks are smoother and less noticeable. To quantify signal distortion and migration rate, we introduced four signal character indicators (ACR, APD, PSR, TR), which outperform previous attack techniques. Additionally, we explored techniques to minimize attack disruption and restrict the impact of the attack.

6   Methodological Comparison

See Table 1.

Table 1. Comparative Analysis

Author Name	Publication with Year	Techniques Used	Dataset Used	Accuracy	Technologies Used	Findings
Xu Han et al. [16]	Wiley Hindawi, 2022	Natural Language Processing (NLP), Deep Neural Network (DNN)	–		Neural network	Text attacks. Adversarial scenarios can inform backdoor attacks, robustness testing, and defense. Readability depends on the objective. Attacks require sophistication. DNN applications will increase the robustness of research
Xiaopeng Fu et al. [17]	Wiley Hindawi, 2021	Visual Similar Word Replacement Algorithm (VSWA)	Yelp Review Dataset and Amazon Review Dataset	Bi-LSTM has 95.64% accuracy and LSTM 95.69 for Yelp Review. For Amazon Review Dataset, LSTM has 88.48% accuracy and BiLSTM 88.55%	Python, LSTM & Bi-LSTM	Utilize the VSWR methodology to generate adversarial instances on datasets utilized for sentiment analysis, thereby launching attacks on pre-trained deep learning classification models
Heng Yin et al. [18]	Wiley Hindawi, 2021	Adam Iterative Fast Gradient	NIPS 2017 Adverarial Competition	95%	Python	In black-box circumstances, including adversarial trained networks, the gradient-based method is superior to gradient-based alternatives. We also targeted an ensemble of networks with novel adversarial example transferability strategies

(continued)

Table 1. (*continued*)

Author Name	Publication with Year	Techniques Used	Dataset Used	Accuracy	Technologies Used	Findings
Murali Krishna Puttagunta et al. [19]	Springer, 2023	Deep Learning Models	MNIST and CIFAR-10		Python	To propose strong medical deep learning implementation decisions. Finally, this paper lists some unsolved research issues that need more research
Yueqiao Li et al. [20]	Elsevier, 2021	AdvCapsNet	CIFAR10	64.14%	Python	To analyze Capsule networks and other basic CNNs against more complicated transfer attacks on two interesting datasets. Offer an AdvCapsNet with AVL for adversarial attack threats. The Capsule network's unified efficiency framework might incorporate the extra loss with regularization losses
Taeyoung Hahn et al. [21]	NeurIPS Proceedings, 2019	Self Routing	CIFAR10, SVHN &SmallNORB	–	Python	Systematic evaluations of our self-routing. Our technique is outstanding at adversarial defense and perspective generalization, CapsNets' strengths. Our technology works better with more capsules per layer than older, inaccurate techniques. CapsNet may not need routing by agreement. Finding a mechanism to add residual connections to our models is interesting because residual networks operate as ensembles of networks with various depths. Our capsules are synergetic

(*continued*)

Table 1. (*continued*)

Author Name	Publication with Year	Techniques Used	Dataset Used	Accuracy	Technologies Used	Findings
Alberto Marchisio et al. [22]	IEEE Access, 2022	Neural Architecture Search algorithm	CIFAR10	86.07%	ROHNAS Framework	Analytical models of DNN and CapsNet layers, activities, visualization, and execution on specialized processors allow architectural modeling and quick hardware estimation. We analyze and select adversarial perturbations to speed up NAS (Neural Architecture Search) robustness evaluation with DNNs. These perturbations highlight DNN discrepancies under adversarial scenarios. We use the Non-dominated Sorting Genetic Algorithm II (NSGA-II) to create an evolutionary algorithm. This technique optimizes DNN adversarial resistance, energy efficiency, memory consumption, and latency via multi-objective Pareto-frontier selection

7 How Do Researchers Evaluate Potential Attacks or Defenses for Adversarial Machine Learning?

This section briefly introduces the basic idea of different defense strategies against adversaries.

7.1 Input Denoising

Adversarial perturbation refers to the introduction of imperceptible noise into data. To prevent this issue, a potential solution is to utilize filtering techniques or incorporate random transformations to counteract the effects of adversarial noise. It is noteworthy that the inclusion of f_x can occur either before the model input layer or as an internal component within the target model.

In the context of the former scenario, where an instance $z*$ is potentially subject to adversarial influence, our objective is to develop a mapping f_x that satisfies the condition $f(f_x(z^*)) = f(z_0)$. In the latter scenario, the concept remains comparable, with the exception that the function f is substituted by the output h of a specific intermediate layer [3].

7.2 Model Robustification

Another commonly utilized strategy is to improve the model's preparation against potential threats from adversaries. There are two potential approaches to improving the model's refinement: altering the training objective or adjusting the model structure. Examples of previous approaches include using adversarial training and substituting real-world training loss with robust training loss. The underlying rationale is to proactively address the potential impact of adversarial samples during a model's training, thereby improving the model's resilience. Instances of model modification encompass various techniques such as model distillation, the implementation of layer discretization, and the regulation of neuron activations. In a formal context, let f^l represent the robust model. The objective is to ensure that $f^l(z*) = f^l(z_0) = y$ [3].

7.3 Adversarial Detection

In contrast to the previous two approaches that attempt to determine the accurate label of a given instance, adversarial detection focuses on determining whether the given instance has been infected by adversarial perturbation. The primary objective is to construct an additional predictor, denoted as fd, which assigns a value of 1 to x if it has been infected and a value of 0 otherwise. The process of establishing fd can be conducted using the conventional approach of constructing a binary classifier. Input denoising and model robustification methods are utilized to prevent the effects of external influences on the accuracy of correction predictions. The adversarial attack involves manipulating the input data and model architectures to achieve the desired outcome. Adversarial detection methods utilize a reactive approach to determine whether the model should proceed with making predictions. To avoid being manipulated, one should be suspicious of the information provided. The implementation of proactive strategies typically presents greater challenges compared to reactive strategies [3].

8   Existing Defense Mechanisms in Adversarial Attack

Existing defense mechanisms have been designed to mitigate the effects of adversarial attacks. These techniques want to improve the robustness of deep learning models, such as capsule networks, against adversarial instances. Here are some common defensive techniques:

1) **Adversarial Training** - Adversarial training is a defensive approach that involves incorporating adversarial instances into the training data. During training, by introducing the model to adversarial disturbances, the model becomes more robust and resistant to such attacks. Adversarial training can enhance the model's accuracy in adversarial instances, but its performance on pure examples may suffer as a result.

2) **Defensive Distillation** - Training a model on reduced logs rather than precise class designations constitutes defensive distillation. Initially, the logs are altered using a temperature parameter, which eliminates the decision boundaries and reduces the model's sensitivity to minor disturbances. This technique has been demonstrated to offer some protection against adversary attacks.

3) **Gradient Masking**- Gradient masking involves obfuscating or concealing the gradients of the model to make it more difficult for adversaries to generate effective adversarial examples. This can be achieved by introducing noise or disturbances into the gradients during backpropagation. Recent research has shown, however, that gradient masking only is not an effective defense.

4) **Ensemble Defense** - Ensemble methods integrate the predictions of multiple models to make more robust decisions. By training multiple models with distinct architectures or random initialization, the ensemble can capture diverse perspectives and mitigate the effects of adversarial attacks. It is less likely that adversarial examples that fool one model will fool the entire ensemble.

5) **Certified Defenses** - Certified defenses provide formal assurances regarding the model's resistance to adversarial attacks. These techniques utilize mathematical checks or bounds to ensure that the model's predictions are robust over a certain range of disturbances. Certified defenses offer more robust guarantees, but they frequently involve additional computational costs.

6) **Input Preprocessing** - Applying input preprocessing techniques, such as input normalization or denoising, can help make the model more resilient to adversarial perturbations. These techniques can reduce the effectiveness of small changes introduced by attackers, making it more difficult to deceive the model [25, 26].

7) **Adversarial Detection and Filtering** - Implementing mechanisms to detect and filter adversarial inputs can help identify potential attacks and prevent them from influencing the model's decisions. This can involve monitoring input data for characteristics indicative of adversarial examples and rejecting or flagging suspicious samples [25, 26].

While these defense mechanisms can provide some protection against adversarial attacks, they may not be universally efficient or applicable in all circumstances. The evolution of adversarial attacks and defense strategies is an ongoing research topic, as is the development of more robust and reliable defense mechanisms against adversarial instances.

9 Existing Research Limitations

Existing research has mainly focused on a limited number of capsule networks, which is one of its primary limitations. Therefore, it is unknown how well the results of this research apply to other capsule networks. Moreover, the majority of research in this field has been conducted with relatively smaller datasets. This makes it challenging to evaluate the resilience of capsule networks against adversarial attacks on large datasets.

Existing research has also been limited by its focus on a relatively small amount of adversarial attacks. Therefore, it is unknown how well the findings of this research apply to other adversarial attacks. In addition, the majority of research in this field has focused on relatively straightforward adversarial attacks. This makes it difficult to evaluate the resilience of capsule networks against more sophisticated adversary attacks.

The majority of research in this field has been focused on developing defenses against adversarial attacks. However, research into the development of methods for identifying adversarial attacks is missing. This is a crucial area of research, as it is possible to create defenses that are efficient against some adversarial attacks but vulnerable to others.

10   How Effective are the Current Defenses Against Adversarial Attacks on Machine Learning Algorithms?

The concerns arising from adversarial attacks are related to the reduction of confidence in the true output class and the possibility of misclassification. The strategies utilized to counter adversarial attacks typically aim to achieve one of two objectives: 1) enhance the ability to be detected the attack, ensuring that clean and malicious inputs can be visually differentiated, or 2) improve the resilience of the deep neural network (DNN) against the attack, thereby minimizing its impact. One potential defense strategy against evasion-based adversarial attacks that are developed using input gradients is to utilize a technique known as gradient masking, which involves minimizing these gradients. The utilization of this technique results in a decrease in the reliability of output classification through the process of retraining the deep neural network (DNN) using the output probability vector. Adversarial training is a frequently utilized defense mechanism in which a trained deep neural network (DNN) undergoes training using adversarial inputs alongside their corresponding correct output labels. This improvement enhances the precision of the system when dealing with a recognized attack.An additional method utilized in the majority of practical machine learning (ML) systems involves the implementation of input pre-processing. The defense mechanism utilized in this scenario involves the process of smoothing, transforming, and reducing the noise before its input into the deep neural network (DNN). This defensive measure reduces adversarial noise, thereby decreasing the likelihood of a successful attack [7].

Adversarial training, a highly effective defense strategy, was proposed as a means for reducing the vulnerability of classification models. This strategy involves the creation and injection of adversarial examples into the training data during the training process. An effective strategy to improve the resilience of segmentation models is the implementation of adversarial training techniques. However, the process of generating efficient segmentation adversarial examples during the training phase can be a time-intensive effort. In this research, we provide proof that shows our SegPGD method is both effective and efficient in addressing this particular challenge. The utilization of SegPGD as the underlying attack method in adversarial training has been found to significantly improve the resilience of segmentation models by generating significant adversarial examples. It is noteworthy to mention that multiple strategies utilizing single-step attacks have been proposed in the context of adversarial training, aiming to address the efficiency of adversarial training in the field of classification. However, single-step attacks do not effectively mislead segmentation models as the adversarial examples they generate are not sufficiently significant [11].

At present, several defense strategies that have been proven effective in countering black-box and gray-box attacks are vulnerable to adaptive white-box attacks. In the 2018 International Conference on Learning Representations (ICLR2018), it was observed that a majority of the heuristic defenses, specifically seven out of nine, were found to be compromised by the adaptive white-box attacks. The application of adversarial attack algorithms, such as Projected Gradient Descent (PGD) and Carlini and Wagner (C&W), to the physical world presents two significant challenges that must be addressed, despite the proven efficiency of these algorithms in the digital domain. One primary challenge is the potential disruption caused by environmental noise and natural transformations, which can compromise the integrity of adversarial perturbations computed in the digital world. The second challenge is related specifically to machine learning tasks that involve images and videos. In these tasks, only the pixels that correspond to specific objects can be altered in the physical world [23].

11 How Do Capsule Neural Networks Differ from Other Types of Neural Networks in Their Susceptibility to Adversarial Attacks? Are There any Current Solutions or Defenses Against Adversarial Attacks on Machine Learning Algorithms?

Capsule Networks can maintain hierarchical spatial relationships among objects, which suggests the possibility of outperforming traditional Convolutional Neural Networks (CNNs) in tasks such as image classification [6].

Convolutional Neural Networks (CNNs) commonly indicate vulnerability to small quasi-imperceptible artificial perturbations, resulting in their vulnerability to being deceived. The vulnerability of convolutional neural networks (CNNs) can present possible risks to applications that prioritize security, such as face verification and autonomous driving. Moreover, the presence of adversarial images serves as evidence that the object recognition mechanism utilized by Convolutional Neural Networks (CNNs) differs significantly from that observed in the human brain. Therefore, there has been a growing interest in adversarial examples since their release [8].

Convolutional neural networks (CNNs) have demonstrated remarkable performance in various domains, emerging as the leading approach. However, recent research revealed a vulnerability in these models, revealing their vulnerability to adversarial perturbations. The presence of gradient calculation instability can contribute to the enhancement of this phenomenon across multiple layers within the network. Nevertheless, it is widely acknowledged that deep neural networks are vulnerable to adversarial inputs, which appear as minimal perturbations introduced to images that are unnoticeable by human observers. Adversarial noise has the potential to deceive convolutional neural networks (CNNs) and other types of neural network architectures, resulting in these models producing inaccurate predictions with a significant level of certainty. The presence of adversarial attacks implements constraints on the utilization of neural networks in tasks that are crucial for security. One possible reason for the efficiency of adversarial samples is that Convolutional Neural Networks (CNNs) show a high degree of linearity within feature spaces of significant dimensionality. While Convolutional Neural Networks (CNNs) can transform feature vectors using non-linear functions, it has been observed that basic activation functions like softmax lack the necessary level of non-linearity to effectively counter adversarial attacks. In contrast, it is worth noting that a Capsule network can generate significantly more complex non-linearities, thereby reducing the vulnerability to adversarial attacks. To address this issue, we present a novel AdvCapsNet model based on Capsule and incorporating a considerably more complicated non-linear function. This model aims to provide robust protection against adversarial attacks [20].

The Capsule network utilizes a dynamic routing mechanism to acquire knowledge about the constituent elements that constitute a particular entity in its entirety. In contrast to deep neural networks, which are limited to modeling local feature knowledge, Capsule networks show the ability to not only model knowledge about local features but also simulate their relationships. Hence, it can be shown that Capsule networks are more effectively designed for image processing, thereby showing superior performance in tasks such as image classification and other related activities. When analyzing the robustness of the Capsule network, it has been observed that it shows greater resilience compared to other frequently utilized neural networks when subjected to certain fundamental white-box adversarial attacks like FGSM and BIM. The Capsule network demonstrates superior classification accuracy compared to general Convolutional Neural Networks (CNNs) in both untargeted and targeted white-box attacks. This indicates that the Capsule network's architecture shows greater effectiveness in terms of adversarial robustness compared to conventional CNN networks [20].

12 Open Challenges and Future Directions

For adversarial attacks and defenses, there are several unresolved issues and potential directions. Among the most significant challenges are:

- *Developing more robust machine learning models* - It is becoming more and more challenging to develop machine learning models that are robust against adversarial attacks as adversarial attacks become more sophisticated.
- *Designing more effective defense mechanisms* - Existing Defense mechanisms are frequently inefficient against evolving and novel adversary attacks. It is crucial to design Defense mechanisms that protect machine learning models from a broad range of adversarial attacks.
- *Understanding the underlying causes of adversarial vulnerability*- The reason machine learning models are vulnerable to adversarial attacks is not yet fully understood. A more in-depth understanding of the fundamental causes of adversarial vulnerability could result in the development of more effective defense mechanisms.

Future research directions in adversarial attacks and defenses include the following:

- *Developing adversarial attack and defense techniques for new machine learning applications*- In the context of image classification, adversarial attacks, and defenses have been extensively investigated. However, it is essential to develop adversarial attack and defense techniques for other applications of machine learning, such as natural language processing and speech recognition.
- *Developing adversarial attack and defense techniques that are robust to real-world conditions* - Typically, laboratory-developed adversarial attacks and Defenses are

not robust under real-world conditions. It is crucial to develop adversarial attack and defense techniques that are resilient to a wide range of real-world scenarios, such as noise, lighting variations, and broad devices.

- *Developing adversarial attack and defense techniques that are efficient and scalable-* Attack and defense techniques that are adversarial can be computationally intensive. It is essential to develop efficient and scalable adversarial attack and defense techniques so that they can be implemented in real-world applications.

The research and analysis of adversarial attacks and defenses is a discipline that is undergoing rapid development. There are many open challenges and potential directions, but there is also a great deal of opportunity for advancement. We can expect the growth of more robust machine learning models and more effective Defense mechanisms as research in this area continues.

13 Conclusion and Future Work

The present state of research on adversarial attacks and defenses in capsule networks is analyzed in this paper. This paper has also discussed the various forms of adversarial attacks that have been proposed, as well as the various defense mechanisms that have been developed to counteract them. And challenges and limitations of existing research, as well as potential directions for future research in this field.

This paper concluded that capsule networks are more robust to adversarial attacks than ordinary neural networks. However, they remain vulnerable to certain forms of attack. There is a need for additional research to develop more efficient defense mechanisms for capsule networks.

This paper also concludes that there is no single defense mechanism that is effective against every type of adversarial attack. It is essential to utilize a combination of defense mechanisms to provide the maximum amount of protection possible against adversarial attacks.

We expect that this review will assist researchers in understanding the challenges and limitations of the existing research on adversarial attacks and defenses in capsule networks. We also expect that this review will assist in the development of more efficient defense mechanisms for capsule networks.

References

1. Kurakin, A., et al.: Adversarial attacks and defenses competition, pp. 195–231 (2018). https://doi.org/10.1007/978-3-319-94042-7_11
2. Qin, Y., Frosst, N., Raffel, C., Cottrell, G., Hinton, G.: Deflecting Adversarial Attacks, no. ICML (2020). http://arxiv.org/abs/2002.07405
3. Liu, N., Du, M., Guo, R., Liu, H., Hu, X.: Adversarial attacks and defenses: an interpretation perspective (2020). http://arxiv.org/abs/2004.11488
4. Marchisio, A., Nanfa, G., Khalid, F., Hanif, M.A., Martina, M., Shafique, M.: SeVuc: a study on the security vulnerabilities of capsule networks against adversarial attacks. Microprocess. Microsyst. **96**, 104738 (2023). https://doi.org/10.1016/j.micpro.2022.104738

5. Osuala, R., et al.: Data synthesis and adversarial networks: a review and meta-analysis in cancer imaging. Med. Image Anal. **84**, 102704 (2023). https://doi.org/10.1016/j.media.2022.102704

6. Marchisio, A., Nanfa, G., Khalid, F., Hanif, M.A., Martina, M., Shafique, M.: CapsAttacks: robust and imperceptible adversarial attacks on capsule networks, pp. 1–10 (2019). http://arxiv.org/abs/1901.09878

7. Shafique, M., et al.: Robust machine learning systems: challenges, current trends, perspectives, and the road ahead. IEEE Des. Test **37**(2), 30–57 (2020). https://doi.org/10.1109/MDAT.2020.2971217

8. Gu, J., Wu, B., Tresp, V.: Effective and efficient vote attack on capsule networks, pp. 1–16 (2021). http://arxiv.org/abs/2102.10055

9. Wu, B., et al.: Attacking adversarial attacks as a defense (2021). http://arxiv.org/abs/2106.04938

10. Sharma, A., Bian, Y., Munz, P., Narayan, A.: Adversarial patch attacks and defenses in vision-based tasks: a survey, pp. 1–15 (2022). http://arxiv.org/abs/2206.08304

11. Jindong, G., Zhao, H., Tresp, V., Torr, P.H.S.: SegPGD: an effective and efficient adversarial attack for evaluating and boosting segmentation robustness. In: Avidan, S., Brostow, G., Cissé, M., Farinella, G.M., Hassner, T. (eds.) Computer Vision – ECCV 2022, Part XXIX, pp. 308–325. Springer, Cham (2022). https://doi.org/10.1007/978-3-031-19818-2_18

12. Marchisio, A., De Marco, A., Colucci, A., Martina, M., Shafique, M.: RobCaps: evaluating the robustness of capsule networks against affine transformations and adversarial attacks, pp. 1–9 (2023). http://arxiv.org/abs/2304.03973

13. Rasheed, B., Khan, A., Ahmad, M., Mazzara, M., Kazmi, S.M.A.: Multiple adversarial domains adaptation approach for mitigating adversarial attacks effects. Int. Trans. Electr. Energy Syst. **2022** (2022). https://doi.org/10.1155/2022/2890761

14. Mao, J., Weng, B., Huang, T., Ye, F., Huang, L.: Research on multimodality face antispoofing model based on adversarial attacks. Secur. Commun. Netw. **2021** (2021). https://doi.org/10.1155/2021/3670339

15. Hu, L., et al.: Transferable adversarial attacks against automatic modulation classifier in wireless communications. Wirel. Commun. Mob. Comput. **2022** (2022). https://doi.org/10.1155/2022/5472324

16. Han, X., Zhang, Y., Wang, W., Wang, B.: Text adversarial attacks and defenses: issues, taxonomy, and perspectives. Secur. Commun. Netw. **2022** (2022). https://doi.org/10.1155/2022/6458488

17. Fu, X., Gu, Z., Han, W., Qian, Y., Wang, B.: Exploring security vulnerabilities of deep learning models by adversarial attacks. Wirel. Commun. Mob. Comput. **2021** (2021). https://doi.org/10.1155/2021/9969867

18. Yin, H., Zhang, H., Wang, J., Dou, R.: Boosting adversarial attacks on neural networks with better optimizer. Secur. Commun. Networks **1**, 2021 (2021). https://doi.org/10.1155/2021/9983309

19. Puttagunta, M.K., Ravi, S., Nelson Kennedy Babu, C.: Adversarial examples: attacks and defenses on medical deep learning systems. Multimed. Tools Appl. (2023). https://doi.org/10.1007/s11042-023-14702-9

20. Li, Y., Su, H., Zhu, J.: AdvCapsNet: to defense adversarial attacks based on Capsule networks. J. Vis. Commun. Image Represent. **75**, 103037 (2021). https://doi.org/10.1016/j.jvcir.2021.103037

21. Hahn, T., Pyeon, M., Kim, G.: Self-routing capsule networks. In: Advances in Neural Information Processing Systems, vol. 32, no. NeurIPS (2019)

22. Marchisio, A., Mrazek, V., Massa, A., Bussolino, B., Martina, M., Shafique, M.: RoHNAS: a neural architecture search framework with conjoint optimization for adversarial robustness

and hardware efficiency of convolutional and capsule networks. IEEE Access **10**, 109043–109055 (2022). https://doi.org/10.1109/ACCESS.2022.3214312

23. Lau, C.P., Liu, J., Lin, W.A., Souri, H., Khorramshahi, P., Chellappa, R.: Adversarial attacks and robust defenses in deep learning. Handb. Stat. **48**, 29–58 (2023). https://doi.org/10.1016/bs.host.2023.01.001

24. Austin Short, A.G., Pay, T.L.: Adversarial examples, DLSS, vol. SAND2019-1, pp. 1–6 (2019). https://www.osti.gov/servlets/purl/1569514

25. Moosavi-Dezfooli, S.M., Fawzi, A., Fawzi, O., Frossard, P.: Universal adversarial perturbations. In: Proceedings - 30th IEEE Conference on Computer Vision and Pattern Recognition, CVPR 2017, vol. 2017-January, pp. 86–94 (2017). https://doi.org/10.1109/CVPR.2017.17

26. Arvidsson, V., Al-Mashahedi, A., Boldt, M.: Evaluation of defense methods against the one-pixel attack on deep neural networks. In: 35th Annual Workshop Swedish Artificial Intelligence Society, SAIS 2023, vol. 199, pp. 49–57 (2023). https://doi.org/10.3384/ecp199005

Control Schemes for Hybrid AC-DC Microgrid

D. Jain$^{(\boxtimes)}$ and D. Saxena

Malaviya National Institute of Technology, Jaipur, India
`2019ree9517@mnit.ac.in`

Abstract. With expanding usage of renewable energy sources, the popularity of microgrids (MG) is also on the rise. Research is ongoing in the field of hybrid MG to develop effective control strategies and stability assessments. Among the three types of MG architecture (AC-coupled, DC-coupled, and hybrid AC-DC coupled), the hybrid AC-DC coupled MG (HACDCMG) is preferred for its benefits. This study focuses on the hierarchical control system of the HACDCMG, which consists of three layers: primary, secondary, and tertiary control. The first one regulates current or voltage, while the secondary control system corrects voltage or current errors and manages power exchange in MG. The tertiary control system manages power sharing along with energy management. The study explores the efficacy of each MG architectural control method, including the coordinated control among multiple ILC and ESS and mode transition. The HACDCMG control method is particularly effective, and this study provides an in-depth analysis of its benefits.

Keywords: Control methods · ESS · Hybrid AC-DC coupled MG · and ILC

Abbreviations

DG: Distributed generators
ESS: Energy storage system
ILC: Interlinking converter
MG: Microgrid
PEC: Power electronic converter
RES: Renewable energy sources
SG: Sub-grid
ADCSG: AC and DC Sub-grid

1 Introduction

The usability of renewable energy sources (RES) is becoming ever more prevalent as a result of a number of factors, including rising demand, scarcity of fuel, decreased air pollution, etc. Therefore, the CERTS, which uses RES like solar, wind, etc., introduces the concept of the microgrid (MG). The major existing utility is connected to various distributed generators (DG) sources with energy storage system (ESS) [1,2] by utilising power electronic converter (PEC). These RES are intermittent, which poses problems with system stability, reliant, etc. Depending on the techno-economic circumstances, the MG may function in either the grid-connected or the islanded mode. Power shortages and surpluses can both exchanged with the primary grid when in the grid-connected mode. According to the IEEE standard IEEE-1547, there are two forms of islanding in the islanded mode: purposeful and inadvertent. Both AC and DC are produced by the main utility grid and by RES. AC loads and sources have been evolving for many years. According to the IEA, energy transmission lost 8 % of all energy in 2021 [3]. Power losses in transmission lines can be decreased and distribution grid power flow can be increased with the help of ACMG. However, additional issues like DER synchronisation and reactive power regulation also appear simultaneously. HVDC transmission systems were employed when the mercury vapour valve was developed in 1930, and this research is bound to high power transmission operations of MG. The usage of diverse loads and DC-DC converters in numerous applications has been made possible by technological and commercial advancements in PEC. Additionally, different ESS types and DC-based DER open up new possibilities for compact DCMG. The primary characteristics of DCMG are its small transformer count and lack of reactive current alternation. After discovering the benefits of both ACMG and DCMG, the development of HACDCMG was the only option left with the purpose of enhancing MG effectiveness, dependability, and financial conditions. Direct fusion of DER, ESS, and AC/DC load is achievable in HACDCMG systems. The HACDCMG eliminates the need for a sizable number of power converters, lowering system costs and losses overall. Due to the synchronisation of the AC and DC buses, the network architecture of the HACDCMG is more complex than that of the scattered AC and DC MG, which necessitates additional research into the coordinated control of the HACDCMG, reactive power compensation, DER disconnection, etc. A hybrid MG's work can be divided into a variety of categories, such as managing the converter to feed best power flow, EMS, system stability, protection etc. The interlinking converter (ILC) must be under control most crucially. ILC regulate the variables v, f, and v at both buses, respectively. Any variation in these particulars will result in the many stability difficulties covered in this work. In

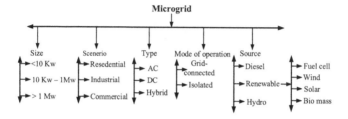

Fig. 1. Overview of MG

review studies, the control method used by ACMG has garnered the majority of attention [4], but DCMG hardly ever classifies all coupling designs and related control techniques. [5] discusses various control strategies for linking AC and DC bus converters. This essay discussed the function of ILC while focusing mostly on control strategies relevant to hybrid MG. The significant findings of this study include:

1. This paper studies the architecture of ACDCMG, and classifying different control strategies in the hierarchical control scheme.
2. It discuss different ILC regulating strategies for ACDCMG architecture.

Following demonstrates how the remaining portion of the paper is organised. The various MG architectures that are available are described in Sect. 2. For an MG architecture that is now available, Sect. 3 offers control approaches. The ILC's function is described in Sect. 4. the discussion of Sect. 5 includes critical reviews. Section 6 brings the paper to a conclusion.

2   Different Architecture of MICROGRID

The term "MG" refers to a mix of DER, controller, and loads. Connections between sources and loads to the PCC can be done in a variety of ways. The hybrid MG architecture is classified into three kinds based on its connections. [6].

2.1   AC Coupled Microgrid

Using its interface converter, it connected DER and SE as shown in Fig. 2. A bidirectional converter connects SEs to the AC bus. Figure 2 explain the AC bus architectural layout. In particular, an optimal control approach along with power flow balance within supply and demand are used to maintain AC bus v, f in islanded mode. Because to its candid design, power management, and control techniques, the ACMG has been a commonly used structure in comparison to other MG architecture for decades.

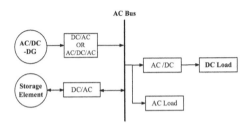

Fig. 2. ACMG Architecture.

2.2   DC Coupled Microgrid

An interface converter connects all of the DER and SE to the DC bus. According to Fig. 3, bidirectional converter connectes the SE's to DC bus. The DCMG does not require complicated wiring and does not require a synchronisation arrangement when merging several DGs (producing DC supply). Furthermore, synchronising the output voltage of parallel IFCs and managing their power can be challenging. Additionally, this network just needs a DC voltage control method.

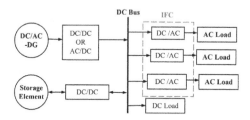

Fig. 3. DCMG Architecture.

2.3   AC-DC Coupled Microgrid

As depicted in Fig. 4, whereas the DC bus is connected to the DC-generated DGs, and the AC bus is associated to the AC-generated DGs. The two buses are connected by the ILC. ILCs serve as bidirectional power converters, transferring power from an AC side to DC side. This tactic is typically taken into account if AC and DC sources and load are available. This architecture considerably increases efficiency by assigning sources and loads to the DC and AC buses with the least amount of power conversion needed. By using fewer power converters, it lowers system expenses. Due to its benefits, it will soon overtake other MG structures as the most promising.

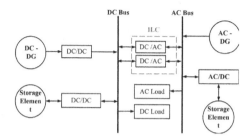

Fig. 4. ACDCMG Architecture.

3   Control Mechanism in AC-DC COUPLED HYBRID MICROGRIDS

Considering that contemporary power networks operate at AC, AC coupled architecture has been the most popular MG design for decades. However, the DCMG is gaining popularity because of advantages including greater usage of sources and loads dependent on DC, fewer synchronisation problems. The HACDCMG is the ideal design as a result since it brings together the benefits of both DC and AC MG. [1,7],. In light of these advantages, the HACDCMG's key problems are stability and power flow management. Numerous studies and reviews have been done on the HACDCMG's stability and control techniques [8]. HACDCMG employ a number of control strategies to obtain the best EMS. The major control issues are stability, power balance, synchronisation, and protection. To accomplish these goals, a sophisticated control system is desired. A hierarchical control structure is largely used in HACDCMG.

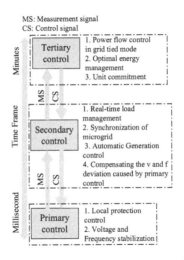

Fig. 5. Block diagram of control mechanism.

3.1   Primary Control

The major control layer is the central component of the HACDCMG's control architecture. This layer is in charge of controlling important variables like v and f. Its major objective is to keep the MG's v and f levels stable. To accomplish this, power flows between the various ESS and DGs connected to the MG are carefully regulated. The grid-following mode and the grid-forming mode are the two main modes of operation used by this layer. While in grid-forming mode, the MG functions independently from the main grid, synchronising its v and f with it. In order to guarantee stable and dependable functioning, the primary control layer is quite important.

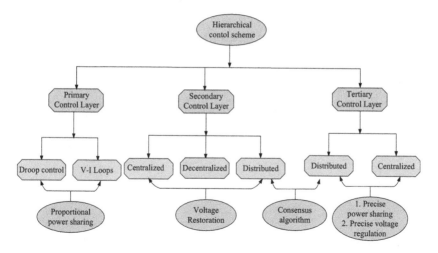

Fig. 6. Hierarchical control structure

3.2 Secondary Control

Building on the foundation of the primary control layer, the secondary control layer adds an extra level of intelligence to the microgrid's management. This layer focuses on compensating for v and f deviations in both the AC and DC sub-grids. Additionally, it ensures smooth transitions between different operating modes, such as black-start and synchronization procedures. There are two main approaches to secondary control: centralized control and decentralized control [9]. In centralized control, a central controller manages power flow distribution based on information gathered from various sources within the microgrid. In decentralized control, individual DGs and ESS units actively participate in power management, allowing for increased reliability in case of system failures [10].

3.3 Tertiary Control

The same control method as during the grid-forming phase is applied here. By regulating the P, Q flows among the HACDCMG, main grid. This method controls v and f. Both centralised and distributed applications of this approach are possible. While p, q are computed using MG power demands and energy market activity, p, q is estimated at the PCC in centralised control. This guarantees the reliability, effectiveness, and affordability of the electricity. In contrast to distributed control, the main grid is used for tertiary control rather than the MGCC. In [11] a HACDCMG design using the tertiary control approach is provided. In this tertiary control technique, global information is acquired via the consensus process. The ideal local choice that takes into account the improvement in power quality is obtained using the optimization procedure. It produces signal of correction for the LC of the DERs in order to boost quality of power at the locak bus. In this control system, the primary controller is given one communication link and for the other link, consensus-based tertiary control is used. These three control mechanisms are summarised in Table 1.

Table 1. Classification based on applications.

Application	Primary	Secondary	Tertiary
Control type	Grid forming	Centralized	Centralized
	Grid following	Decentralized	Distributed
	Local	Global and local	Global
Connectivity	Both islanded and grid connected mode	Both islanded and grid-connected mode	Islanded mode
Complexity	Less	More	More
Cost	Less	More	More

4   ILC Control Methods

It can control separate SG with more flexibility by commanding connected converters dispersed throughout MG to carry out different functions. The most popular method is to use these converters to reduce v/f variability in ac and dc SG [1,2,12]. In order to counterbalance any surplus produced or needed power on each networks, the converters would transmit electricity through one SG to another. It's not necessary for this functioning mechanism to be restricted to ac and dc SG along with a similar voltage, frequency level. It could also be employed when the v and f levels are different but the current attributes are similar. With the aid of a droop controller, ILC can transfer power among a MG's SG. In addition to conventional techniques, this droop is calculated using the differential among their AC SG f variance and their DC SG v variance. These variations differ from one another, so the HACDCMG converters supply power to stabilise them. The ILC's capacity determines the amount of power sharing that can be transmitted in both directions between AC and DC buses. It's important to keep in mind that even though ILCs associated to the AC grid provide local primary regulations. They are not eligible to be added to the main resource. This is because they switch power between grids rather than supplying or dissipating energy from a source or a load. Additionally, an ILC can assist with primary regulation on both sides in specific situations, anytime one of the SG has surplus generating electricity, for instance and an adjacent system requires a high amount of power. By moving power from one system to the other, ILC aid in the regulation of both systems in this instance. Even yet, one SG will profit from the primary regulation while the other will experience a bigger variance If two sub-grids have insufficient power generation or demand, and ILC is in charge of handling the deviation compensation. Other methods can be utilised to control the ILC implemented at MG, such as SoC balancing of ESSs or enhancing energy quality. Dynamic droop characteristics make it difficult to reconcile the droop variables of different DERs, and any DER could be shut down for maintenance [13]. Classical Droop based on DC voltage for the HACDCMG ILC outgrowth circulating current as a result of different line resistances that put the ILC under excessive stress. In [14], "frequency-based droop is described as a way to prevent power from being circulated between various ILCs. The ADCSG own their own ESS in HACDCMG setups that are currently in use. Owing to the substantial volume of power exchange and the numerous links among the ADCSG, numerous ILCs are provided in [15]. We'll go over some of the most crucial ILC control tactics in the following section.

4.1 ILC Unified Control

An inner v/f loop and an external power control loop are included in the control block diagram of this method in [15]. The DERs and ESS are separated into two groups on either side: power and slack terminals. Power balancing units, also known as slack terminals, are DERs-ESSs on the ADCSG that are employed to control f and the v of the ADCSG, whereas power terminals on AC and DC SG are DERs-ESSs that try to run in MPPT mode. Assume that the ADCSG power terminals' combined total outputs are P_{ac} and P_{dc}, correspondingly, assuming that the following are the droop characteristics:

$$V_{dc} = V_{dc}^* + (P_{dc}^* - P_{dc})/K_{dc} \tag{1}$$

$$\omega_{ac} = \omega_{ac}^* + (P_{ac}^* - P_{ac})/K_{ac} \tag{2}$$

where, for a DC SG, $V_{dc}, V_{dc}^*, K_{dc}, P_{dc}^*$ and P_{dc} are, respectively, voltage at the slack bus terminal, reference voltage for the DC bus, gain for DC droop, reference real power for the DC bus, and the momentary active power. The same is true for $\omega_{ac}, \omega_{ac}^*, K_{ac}, P_{ac}^*$ and P_{ac}, which stand for the instantaneous p of the ac SG, reference active power, slack bus frequency, and reference frequency, respectively. In typical operation, the PCC's overall actual power output of the ADCSG is endured using the potential (K). The power error (ΔP) PCC is displayed as:

$$\delta_P = P_{ac} - K * P_{dc} \tag{3}$$

When determining the real power reference set-point, the regulator transfer function G(s) can be used to estimate the base output power shown in Fig. 6 using the Eqs. 1, 2, 3. As a result, AC voltage control is used, and monitoring is done with a PR controller, which additionally diminishes steady-state error and enhances dynamic stability.

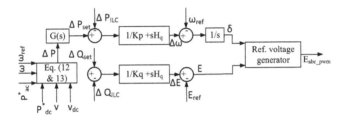

Fig. 7. ILC unified control structure.

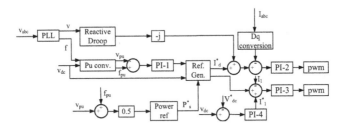

Fig. 8. ESS with ILC control structure.

4.2 ILC with ESS

The [1] presents a novel HACDCMG layout that integrates ESS into the ILC. Energy could be stored using the system of batteries or capacitors at the DC link of the ILC. ESS and ILC are associated to the DC SG via a DC-DC boost converter, and to the AC SG via a DC-AC converter. The storage system and ILCs system model are shown together in Fig. 8. By using PLL, V_{abc} is transformed to v, f, which are then converted to values per unit. Making use of per-unit system parameters, it is possible to rule out the control error caused by distinct droop gains caused by line and system factors. According to 4, 5, (f_{pu}), (V_{pu}) are defined.

$$f_{p.u.} = \frac{f - 1/2(f_{max} + f_{min})}{1/2(f_{max} - f_{min})} \tag{4}$$

$$V_{p.u.} = \frac{V - 1/2(V_{max} + V_{min})}{1/2(V_{max} - V_{min})} \tag{5}$$

The PI-I controller gets the p.u. v and f deception and yields a real power reference signal (P_1^*). The actual power reference signal determines the real power transmission among ADCSG. Following that, using the 6, 7, the active current reference (I_d^*) and the DC current reference (I_1^*) are measured from (P_1^*).

$$I_d^* = \frac{2P_1^*}{3V} \tag{6}$$

$$I_q^* = \frac{-2Q_1^*}{3V} \tag{7}$$

I_1^* is DC side current and $I_d^* + jI_q^*$ are ILC's AC side current, controlled through PI-2 and PI-3. The PI-4 controller's function is to maintain a constant voltage across the DC link capacitor, allowing the use of an ILC in place of a capacitor. However, charging and discharging of ESS depends on the v of DC bus.

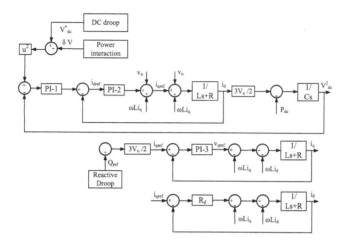

Fig. 9. Bidirectional ILC control structure.

4.3   Multiple Bidirectional ILCs Control

In [16], using a distributed coordination control across several simultaneous ILCs is proposed in a HACDCMG, and ILC and ESS are associated among the ADCSG. Among the existing control techniques described in [17–20] and this approach in [16], there are significant differences in the three-axis dq_o control over the feedback linearization technique and the BILCs' internal current loop. Moreover, normalised (per-unit) f/DC v droop is used to achieve power interaction. A circulating current can be created by many parallel-connected ILCs, but this current is suppressed by the [21,22]. On the other hand, a decoupling controller is developed employing a DC SG voltage-based evaluation strategy. A thorough control strategy for multiple ILCs with three axes of the inner current loop is shown in Fig. 9. Such two coupled control strategies significantly improve ILC active power sharing, ILC inner current management, and ESS stress reduction via creating reactive power. Power management, which controls Power interaction and DC current sharing between ADCSG, is frequently controlled by the outer control loop. The power interaction is as follows:

$$V_{dc,ref} = V_{dc}^* - \delta V - R_k(i_{dc} - i_{dc}^*) \tag{8}$$

$$Q_{ref} = Q - N_k(V_u - V_u^*) \tag{9}$$

where, i_{dc}^* output current, $V_{(dc,ref)}$, the reference DC link voltage, the output of power interaction control is $\delta V = K(f_{ref} - f)$, and R_k droop coefficient.

5 Critical Review

HACDCMG have gained popularity as the most common MG architecture because of its numerous advantages, including increased reliability, efficacy, and affordability of the system. There are several issues in this area that need to be looked into.

Table 2. Comparison of ILC Control Strategies

Control Strategy	Key Features	Advantages	Considerations
ILC Unified Control	1) Utilizes per-unit system parameters for control accuracy. 2) Active and reactive current regulation through PI controllers.	1) Effective power sharing between SGs. 2) Reduced steady-state error. 3) Enhances dynamic stability.	1) Sensitive to line impedance mismatch. 2) Requires accurate parameter tuning. 3) Limited adaptability for dynamic SGs.
ILC with ESS	1) Incorporates Energy Storage Systems (ESS) into ILC. 2) Uses per-unit system parameters and control loops for ILC and ESS. 3) Balances charging and discharging of ESS with v/f control.	1) Improved DC link voltage stability. 2) Reduced voltage fluctuations. 3) Enhanced dynamic stability.	1) ESS state of charge (SoC) management. 2) Proper ESS control strategy needed. 3) Dependent on ESS characteristics.
Multiple Bidirectional ILCs Control	1) Coordination of parallel-connected ILCs with three-axis dqo control. 2) Feedback linearization technique and per-unit f/DC v droop. 3) Controls power interaction between AC and DC SGs.	1) Improved active power sharing. 2) Enhanced ILC inner current management. 3) ESS stress reduction.	1) Complex control algorithm. 2) Additional computational complexity. 3) Circulating current suppression

1. It is necessary to conduct farther research on coordinated control methods for AC and DC bus power sharing in additionally to individual SG because HACDCMGs have more intricate power sharing strategy in contrast to isolated AC and DC MGs.
2. Due to the HACDCMG's reliance on the ILC for power exchange among the buses, BILCs are necessary for stability. In addition, depending on the HACDCMG's working mode, either the AC bus v/f or the DC bus v will be regulated by the BILC.
3. A large number of ILCs are used with the AC and DC bus due to the high quantity of Power exchange between the two buses. As a result, adding more ILCs would enhance overall expenses and lead to circulating current because

of a line's mismatched impedance, that might put the ILCs below undue pressure.

4. The control technique of numerous ILCs is essential due to the insertion of distributed ESSs on the AC and DC SG. Therefore, more investigation is needed to create a control approach between several ILCs that run in parallel and distributed ESSs.
5. The major issue is the regulation of distributed ESSs' charging and discharging at varied SoC levels. For distributed ESSs with several SoC levels, the master-slave control technique was employed the majority of the time; however, only a few studies emphasised on balancing the SoC levels of decentralized ESSs.
6. The entire MG will be shut down if the MGCC in the communication infrastructure malfunctions. Yet, because the dependability of the MG can be increased via distributed control systems, which lack an MGCC and permit the LC of numerous DERs to converse with each other.

Future MG will eventually cluster together to produce complex dynamics as they become more and more coupled with one another. By enabling policymakers, the power sector enables both industry practitioners and academic scholars to grasp the stability, and power management scenarios of different MG systems.

6   Conclusion

This study provides a thorough literature review of control techniques for HACD-CMG. While previous research has explored various aspects of MG, current academic and industrial focus is on control strategies, which are crucial for the successful implementation of MG. The control hierarchy for all architecture is defined in a similar way, with primary control handling constant v/f and power regulation, and secondary and tertiary control addressing distinct operating modes. The DER incorporates the primary layer to enhance reliability, and alongside this, the secondary layer optimizes power quality by governing MG communication protocols and mitigating steady-state v/f faults. To facilitate efficient operation, the tertiary control supervises power distribution between the MG and the main grid. The advantages of various control strategies for ILCs have been thoroughly examined in this research. The efficient management of ILCs is closely related to the system's stability. The voltage levels on both the AC and DC buses, for instance, may be dramatically affected in situations when numerous ILCs are used and there is a high circulating current flowing between them. Using ILCs in conjunction with ESS is one efficient way to deal with this circulating current issue.

References

1. Loh, P.C., Li, D., Chai, Y.K., Blaabjerg, F.: Autonomous operation of hybrid microgrid with AC and DC subgrids. IEEE Trans. Power Electron. **28**(5), 2214–2223 (2012)

2. Baharizadeh, M., Karshenas, H.R., Guerrero, J.M.: Control strategy of interlinking converters as the key segment of hybrid ac-dc microgrids. IET Generation, Trans. Distrib. **10**(7), 1671–1681 (2016)
3. Yang, Y., Yang, P.: A novel strategy for improving power quality of islanded hybrid ac/dc microgrid using parallel-operated interlinking converters. Int. J. Electr. Power Energy Syst. **138**, 107961 (2022)
4. Han, H., Hou, X., Yang, J., Wu, J., Su, M., Guerrero, J.M.: Review of power sharing control strategies for islanding operation of ac microgrids. IEEE Trans. Smart Grid **7**(1), 200–215 (2015)
5. Zolfaghari, M., Gharehpetian, G.B., Shafie-khah, M., Catalão, J.P.: Comprehensive review on the strategies for controlling the interconnection of AC and DC microgrids. Int. J. Electr. Power Energy Syst. **136**, 107742 (2022)
6. Che, L., Shahidehpour, M., Alabdulwahab, A., Al-Turki, Y.: Hierarchical coordination of a community microgrid with ac and dc microgrids. IEEE Trans. smart grid **6**(6), 3042–3051 (2015)
7. Eghtedarpour, N., Farjah, E.: Power control and management in a hybrid AC/DC microgrid. IEEE Trans. Smart Grid **5**(3), 1494–1505 (2014)
8. Nutkani, I.U., Loh, P.C., Wang, P., Blaabjerg, F.: Cost-prioritized droop schemes for autonomous ac microgrids. IEEE Trans. Power Electron. **30**(2), 1109–1119 (2014)
9. Katiraei, F., Iravani, M.R., Lehn, P.W.: Micro-grid autonomous operation during and subsequent to islanding process. IEEE Trans. Power Delivery **20**(1), 248–257 (2005)
10. Li, H., Shi, K., McLaren, P.: Neural-network-based sensorless maximum wind energy capture with compensated power coefficient. IEEE Trans. Ind. Appl. **41**(6), 1548–1556 (2005)
11. Che, L., Shahidehpour, M.: Dc microgrids: economic operation and enhancement of resilience by hierarchical control. IEEE Trans. Smart Grid **5**(5), 2517–2526 (2014)
12. Gao, F., et al.: Comparative stability analysis of droop control approaches in voltage-source-converter-based dc microgrids. IEEE Trans. Power Electron. **32**(3), 2395–2415 (2016)
13. Radwan, A.A.A., Mohamed, Y.A.R.I.: Bidirectional power management in hybrid ac-dc islanded microgrid system. In: 2014 IEEE PES General Meeting— Conference & Exposition, pp. 1–5. IEEE, (2014)
14. Peyghami, S., Mokhtari, H., Blaabjerg, F.: Autonomous operation of a hybrid AC/DC microgrid with multiple interlinking converters. IEEE Trans. Smart Grid **9**(6), 6480–6488 (2017)
15. Li, X., Guo, L., Li, Y., Guo, Z., Hong, C., Zhang, Y., Wang, C.: A unified control for the dc-ac interlinking converters in hybrid ac/dc microgrids. IEEE Trans. Smart Grid **9**(6), 6540–6553 (2017)
16. Xia, Y., Peng, Y., Yang, P., Yu, M., Wei, W.: Distributed coordination control for multiple bidirectional power converters in a hybrid ac/dc microgrid. IEEE Trans. Power Electron. **32**(6), 4949–4959 (2016)
17. Guerrero, J.M., Vasquez, J.C., Matas, J., De Vicuña, L.G., Castilla, M.: Hierarchical control of droop-controlled ac and dc microgrids-a general approach toward standardization. IEEE Trans. Industr. Electron. **58**(1), 158–172 (2010)
18. Bidram, A., Davoudi, A., Lewis, F.L., Guerrero, J.M.: Distributed cooperative secondary control of microgrids using feedback linearization. IEEE Trans. Power Syst. **28**(3), 3462–3470 (2013)

19. De Brabandere, K., Bolsens, B., Van den Keybus, J., Woyte, A., Driesen, J., Belmans, R.: A voltage and frequency droop control method for parallel inverters. IEEE Trans. Power Electron. **22**(4), 1107–1115 (2007)
20. Zhong, Q.-C.: Robust droop controller for accurate proportional load sharing among inverters operated in parallel. IEEE Trans. Industr. Electron. **60**(4), 1281–1290 (2011)
21. Espinoza, J.R., Joós, G.: State variable decoupling and power flow control in pwm current-source rectifiers. IEEE Trans. Industr. Electron. **45**(1), 78–87 (1998)
22. Blasko, V., Kaura, V.: A novel control to actively damp resonance in input lc filter of a three-phase voltage source converter. IEEE Trans. Ind. Appl. **33**(2), 542–550 (1997)

Design of Low Power and Energy Efficient Write Driver with Bitline Leakage Compensation for SRAM

Monica Gupta$^{(\boxtimes)}$, Kirti Gupta , and Monica Bhutani

Department of Electronics and Communication Engineering, Bharati Vidyapeeth's
College of Engineering, New Delhi, India
monica.gupta@bharatividyapeeth.edu

Abstract. High performance applications demand faster SRAM with low power and energy consumption, wherein the write driver is a critical component governing its write performance. The existing write drivers fail to optimize all the parameters simultaneously due to bitline leakage-discharge current trade-off. In this paper, a novel write driver is presented, which uses a unique leakage-compensation mechanism to overcome this trade-off. The designs are implemented at 32 nm and are compared under PVT-variations with 3σ global process and frequency variations. The results show that the proposed design outdo all the existing designs, providing up to a 9.9% improvement in write delay, with a 26.75%, 26.03% and 29.13% reduction in write power, energy per switching activity, and differential bitline voltage, respectively, at 1.1 V, 27 °C and TT corner. Thus, the design is suitable for a multitude of applications due to its low write delay, reduced power consumption and increased energy efficiency.

Keywords: PVT-variations · write delay · bitline leakages ·
leakage-compensation · write power · write driver · energy per switching
activity · SRAM

1 Introduction

The interest in incorporating additional features in high performance applications and portable devices requires a large amount of SRAM in a small chip area [1, 2]. SRAM has become so popular due to its faster speed and high storage density [3]. The speed of operation in SRAM is mainly dictated by the performance of its peripheral circuitry. Thus, SRAM array architecture with an efficient write driver, sense amplifier, decoders, multiplexers, etc., improves the overall system performance [4, 5]. An efficient write driver design aiming for faster write operations requires a large differential bitline voltage and high discharge current. However, the high bitline leakages of unselected SRAM cells and write driver along the column reduce the differential bitline voltage. Stacking of transistors is an effective way to reduce the bitline leakages [6]. Although this reduces leakages and power consumption, the detrimental effect on discharge current has made the design of write driver with a smaller write delay challenging.

R. C. Bansal et al. (Eds.): ACTET 2023, CCIS 2000, pp. 48–64, 2024.
https://doi.org/10.1007/978-3-031-54162-9_4

Given its significant contribution to the total power usage in SRAM arrays, optimizing write power directly reduces overall consumption, while simultaneously increased bitline voltages enhance cell reliability during write operations. To provide improved write performance, various write driver designs are available, such as the constant-negative level write driver [7], mirrored write driver [8], pass-gate based write driver [9, 10], transmission-gate based write driver [11], AND-gate based write driver [11], and NOR-gate based write driver [12, 13]. The constant-negative level write driver [7] and mirrored write driver [8] make use of negative bitline assist technique and current mirror circuit, respectively, to improve write performance. However, the use of large boost capacitor and maintenance of a precise value of the reference current in these designs make them less attractive. The pass-gate based write driver [9, 10] has the advantage of low power consumption; however, it suffers from poor write delay due to reduced discharge current. The AND-gate based write driver [11] provides a slight improvement in write delay values but suffers from increased bitline leakages, resulting in a deteriorated differential voltage between the bitlines. The transmission-gate based write driver [11] suffers from increased energy consumption. Moreover, the performance in AND-gate, pass-gate, and transmission-gate based write drivers degrades due to trade-off between bitline leakages and discharge current. The NOR-gate based write driver [12, 13] proves to be a better alternative to these designs, but the increased write power and energy consumption makes it a less desirable option given the recent demand for low power devices. Thus, there is a need to propose a new write driver design that can address the issues of existing designs and provide faster and more efficient write operations with reduced write power and energy consumption.

In this work, a novel design for a write driver is proposed. The design exhibits faster writing with reduced power and energy consumption. The contributions of this work are summarized as follows:

- The design overcomes the trade-off between bitline leakages and discharge current; a major concern in existing designs.
- It employs a leakage-compensation control circuitry that compensates for the bitline leakage currents of the unselected SRAM cells and the write driver, helping to maintain a large differential voltage between the bitlines.
- The use of stacking effect in the core structure and the requirement for a lesser number of transistors for implementation reduce power and energy consumption, as well as area overhead.
- The presence of only one pass transistor in the discharge path of the bitline facilitates faster discharging and reduces write delay.

This paper is organized as follows. Section 2 discusses the working of an SRAM cell in an SRAM architecture and the issue pertinent to bitline leakages and discharge current. In Sect. 3, existing write driver designs and the issues related to their performance are discussed. Section 4 presents the structure of the proposed write driver design and explains its working. Simulation results are presented and discussed in Sect. 5. Finally, concluding remarks are discussed in Sect. 6 of the paper.

2 SRAM Cell and Array Architecture

SRAM array architecture consists of a matrix of cells with various peripherals connected to a column or a row of SRAM cells for performing memory operations. Each cell can store either '1' or '0'. A column of SRAM cells along with the peripherals (such as pre-charge circuit, write driver etc.) required for performing the write access can be seen in Fig. 1. A pre-charge circuit employs pMOS transistors and is driven by control signal PC [9]. The SRAM cell selected for write operation comprises of two cross-coupled CMOS inverters (pull-up transistors: PU1-PU2, pull-down transistors: PD1-PD2) and two access transistors (A12, A22) driven by word line WL2. The access transistors connect the internal nodes (W2 and WB2) to the complementary bitlines BL and BLB, which in turn have parasitic capacitances C_{BL} and C_{BLB} respectively. The cell can be made to operate in: hold mode, write mode, read mode [10]. The write driver is controlled by data input D_IN and write enable control signal WE.

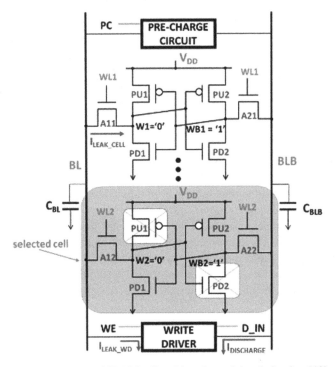

Fig. 1. A column of SRAM cells with write peripheral circuitry [10]

2.1 Write Operation in Cell

Each write access cycle consists of a pre-charge phase (first half cycle) followed by a write operation (next half cycle). To illustrate the complete cycle, it is assumed that the cell stores '0' at node W2 and write '1' operation is to be carried out. In the first half of cycle, signal PC is pulled low in the pre-charge circuit and the bitline capacitors are charged to V_{DD}. In the next half cycle, PC is disabled and one-bit data is applied through data input D_IN. Next, the signal WE is enabled in the write driver that results in discharging of bitline capacitor C_{BLB} and flow of discharge current $I_{DISCHARGE}$. After this, the access transistors are turned ON in the selected cell by pulling the wordline WL2 high. The write operation begins at node storing '1' that is node WB2 in this case. A large discharging current starts flowing through A22 against the charging current through PU2. For a successful write operation, thus, a stronger access transistor is required compared to pull-up transistor. Concurrently, at node W2 a charging current through A12 also increases the voltage at W2. The write operation is accomplished when the voltage at WB2 falls below the switching threshold voltage of PU1-PD1 inverter and node voltages at W2 and WB2 flip. In a similar manner, the write '1' operation is also carried out in the selected cell. It is worth mentioning that a large differential voltage between BL and BLB (Δ_{BL}) and a high magnitude discharge current ($I_{DISCHARGE}$) is required for smaller write delay (T_{WD}). However, as soon as the PC signal turns high during second half cycle, then due to the flow of bitline leakage currents I_{LEAK_CELL} and I_{LEAK_WD} in unselected SRAM cells and write driver respectively along the column of the SRAM array, the BL voltage reduces, decreasing the differential voltage between the bitlines. This in turn results in reduced flow of currents through the access transistors of the selected SRAM cell during the writing process. In addition, the stacking of transistors in the discharge path of bitlines reduces the strength of $I_{DISCHARGE}$ further deteriorating the write delay (T_{WD}). Thus, for improved write performance it is imperative to address increased bitline leakages (I_{LEAK_CELL} and I_{LEAK_WD}) and reduced discharge current ($I_{DISCHARGE}$) while maintaining power (P_W) and energy (E_W) consumption low.

3 Previous Write Drivers

A write driver strongly affects the write performance of the memory; hence, a design that can discharge the pre-charged bitline quickly while simultaneously maintaining power and energy consumption low is in high demand. Some of the existing designs are discussed next [9–13].

3.1 Pass-Gate based (PG) Write Driver [9, 10]

Figure 2(a) shows the schematic of PG [9] design, wherein the pass transistors (M1-M4) and inverters (I1-I2) are controlled by signals WE and D_IN. One of the pre-charged bitline conditionally discharges to ground during write operation when WE turns high. The design is popular due to its simplicity and low power consumption. However, it suffers from reduced $I_{DISCHARGE}$ due to the stacking of two pass transistors in the discharging path of the bitline, deteriorating T_{WD}. It is worth mentioning that the stacking effect helps in suppressing one component of bitline leakage current I_{LEAK_WD} existing in other branch while the other leakage component I_{LEAK_CELL} remains unaddressed. Thus, the performance suffers due to the trade-off between bitline leakages and discharge current.

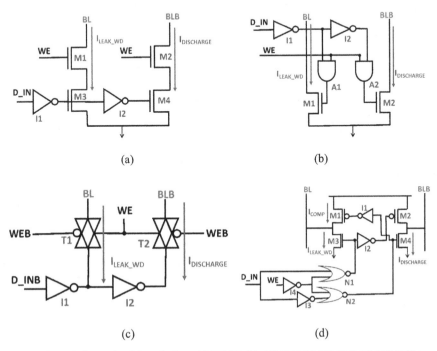

(a)

(b)

(c)

(d)

Fig. 2. Existing write driver designs (a) PG [9] (b) AG [11] (c) TG [11] (d) NG [12]

3.2 AND-Gate based (AG) Write Driver [11]

The AG write driver design depicted in Fig. 2(b) incorporates AND gates A1 and A2 for cutting-down the transistor count in the discharging path and enabling comparatively faster write operation. One of the discharge path through either M1 or M2 is enabled during write operation as per the output of AND gates. The effective ON resistance of the discharge path is reduced as now only one transistor is present in each path in comparison to PG [9] design thus increasing $I_{DISCHARGE}$ and resulting in slightly improved T_{WD}. However, the design fails to address the issue of increased bitline leakages I_{LEAK_WD} and I_{LEAK_CELL} and thus suffers from deteriorated Δ_{BL} due to the trade-off between bitline leakages and discharge current.

3.3 Transmission-Gate Based (TG) Write Driver[11]

Figure 2(c) represents TG [11] write driver design (Fig. 2(c)) wherein transmission gates (T1, T2) and inverters (I1, I2) are employed to conditionally discharge the bitlines. The transmission gates and inverters are driven by control signals WE, its compliment WEB and compliment of data input D_INB. During write operation, when WE and WEB turns high and low respectively, the transmission gates are enabled and one of the bit-line conditionally discharges through nMOS transistor of inverter (either I1 or I2). The quick discharging of high capacitive bitlines require inverters with strong nMOS transistor. The stacking effect of transmission gate and strong inverter reduces $I_{DISCHARGE}$ and results in large T_{WD} and increased energy consumption. In addition, the design requires extra inverters to generate control signals WEB and D_INB from WE and D_IN respectively. Moreover, the design suppresses I_{LEAK_WD} whereas the I_{LEAK_CELL} remains unaddressed resulting in degraded Δ_{BL}.

3.4 NOR-Gate based (NG) Write Driver [12, 13]

The NG [12] design (Fig. 2(d)) consists of transistor pairs (M1-M4, M2-M3), NOR gates (N1, N2) and inverters (I1, I2, I3, I4). During write operation, WE turns high and output of either N1 or N2 comes to be high based on the value of D_IN. This results in triggering of one of the pair either M2-M3 or M1-M4. In each pair, pull-down transistor is used to discharge the bitline by means of $I_{DISCHARGE}$ whereas pull-up transistor keeps the other bitline high through compensation current I_{COMP}. The reverse flow of I_{COMP} through M1 compensates for the leakage currents I_{LEAK_CELL} and I_{LEAK_WD} improving Δ_{BL}. However, the proposal uses huge number of transistors and, thus, suffers from increased write power and energy consumption, and area overhead.

In the existing write driver designs (Fig. 2), it can be observed that it is not possible to provide a small write delay (T_{WD}) at low power and energy consumption due to the trade-off between bitline leakages (I_{LEAK_CELL} and I_{LEAK_WD}) and discharge current ($I_{DISCHARGE}$). The AG [11] design improves $I_{DISCHARGE}$ but suffers from degraded values of Δ_{BL} due to more bitline leakages. In PG [9] and TG [11] designs, the use of stacking effect helps in reducing only the leakage current component I_{LEAK_WD} while the other more critical leakage current component I_{LEAK_CELL} remains unaddressed. Moreover, the stacking effect reduces $I_{DISCHARGE}$ and thus deteriorates T_{WD}. In addition, the TG [11] design suffers from increased energy consumption. The NG [12] design overcomes this trade-off to a certain extent but suffers from increased write power and energy consumption. Thus, the existing write driver designs focus on I_{LEAK_WD} but at the cost of limitation on $I_{DISCHARGE}$. In addition, I_{LEAK_CELL} of unselected SRAM cells remains unaddressed. Hence, the existing designs are not suitable for portable devices and high performance applications that need faster write in addition to low power and energy consumption. This necessitates a new write driver design that can optimize all the performance parameters by overcoming the trade-off between bitline leakages and discharge current while simultaneously addressing the issue of increased write power P_W and energy consumption E_W.

4 Proposed Write Driver Design

The existing write driver designs discussed in Sect. 3, suffer from the issue of poor T_{WD} values, deteriorated Δ_{BL}, high P_W and E_W consumptions that worsens with supply and technology scaling. To address these issues a novel design for a write driver is proposed. The proposed design overcomes the trade-off between bitline leakages (I_{LEAK_CELL} and I_{LEAK_WD}) and discharge current ($I_{DISCHARGE}$) while keeping the P_W and E_W consumptions low.

4.1 Structure of the Proposed Write Driver

The proposed write driver design incorporates a unique leakage-compensation mechanism that provides compensation against bitline leakage currents I_{LEAK_CELL} and I_{LEAK_WD} of the unselected SRAM cells and write driver respectively resulting in large Δ_{BL}. The use of stacking effect in the core structure and the requirement of lesser number of transistors for implementation reduces the power and energy consumption, and area overhead. The presence of only one pass transistor in the discharge path of bitline fosters faster discharging due to flow of high magnitude $I_{DISCHARGE}$ and, thus, reduces T_{WD}.

The SRAM array architecture consisting of pre-charge circuit, conventional 6T SRAM cell and the proposed write driver design is shown in Fig. 3(a). The pre-charge circuit is regulated by a control signal PC. The selected cell stores the data at the internal storage nodes W2 and WB2, which in turn are connected to the external bitlines BL and BLB through the access transistors A12 and A22 respectively. The access transistors are driven by word line WL2. The proposed write driver design consists of pull-up transistors (M1, M2, M3, M4), pull-down transistors (M5, M6) and AND gates (A1, A2). The inverters are also required to get the complementary signals D_INB and WEB from D_IN and WE respectively that controls the overall working of the write driver. The control signals WEB and WE respectively keep the pull-up path (M1-M3 or M2-M4) for I_{COMP} and pull-down path (M5 or M6) for $I_{DISCHARGE}$ disabled during pre-charge phase and conditionally turns one of the pull-up and pull-down paths ON during write operation.

4.2 Working Mechanism

The timing diagram shown in Fig. 3(b) represents the value of various signals and critical nodes while performing memory access in selected SRAM cell. Each memory access consists of a pre-charge half cycle followed by a read or write half cycle depending upon the value of RD/WR control signal. Now, let us see the working of the circuit during write '1' access in reference to the signal values depicted in Fig. 3(c). During the pre-charge half cycle, the WE and PC signals turn low in write driver and pre-charge circuit respectively and results in pre-charging of bitlines to V_{DD}. As WE is low, both the AND gates are disabled irrespective of the value of D_IN. This keeps both the pull-down transistors (M5 and M6) OFF and helps the bitlines to hold the pre-charged voltage. During write '1' half cycle, signals WE and WEB turn high and low respectively. Now the output of the AND gates depend upon the data applied at data input D_IN. During write '1' operation, D_IN is high and therefore the output of AND gate A2 becomes '1' whereas A1 remains '0'. The transistor M6 quickly discharges the bitline BLB towards ground resulting in the flow of discharge current $I_{DISCHARGE}$. On the other hand, M1 and M3 keep BL voltage high. This occurs due to the flow of compensation current I_{COMP} through M1 and M3 that compensates for the bitline leakage currents I_{LEAK_CELL} and I_{LEAK_WD} of the unselected SRAM cells and nMOS transistor M5 of the write driver respectively. Thus, a large Δ_{BL} is maintained resulting in flow of large currents through access transistors of selected SRAM cell during write operation. In addition, the presence of only one transistor M6 in the discharge path of BLB results in high $I_{DISCHARGE}$. A large Δ_{BL} and high magnitude $I_{DISCHARGE}$ simultaneously work to improve T_{WD}. The reduced transistor count and presence of stacking effect in the core structure leads to low write power and energy consumption in the proposed design. The write '0' operation is also performed in a similar way. Thus, the proposed design successfully overcomes the drawbacks of existing designs and provides faster write at low power and energy consumption.

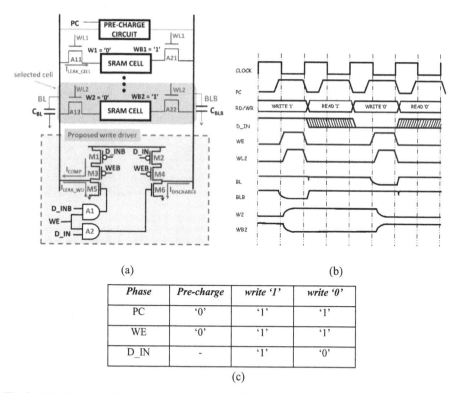

(a)   (b)

Phase	Pre-charge	write '1'	write '0'
PC	'0'	'1'	'1'
WE	'0'	'1'	'1'
D_IN	-	'1'	'0'

(c)

Fig. 3. SRAM array with proposed write driver (a) Circuit diagram (b) Timing diagram depicting read/write operation (c) Status of control signals during write '1' and write '0' operations

4.3 Bitline Leakage-Compensation

To ensure a faster and successful write operation, it is required to maintain a large Δ_{BL}. However, due to the flow of bitline leakage currents I_{LEAK_CELL} and I_{LEAK_WD} through the unselected SRAM cells and write driver respectively along the column of an SRAM array, this becomes difficult. The problem further exaggerates with supply and technology scaling. To address this issue in the proposed design, a leakage-compensation circuitry is used that compensates for the bitline leakage currents through I_{COMP} and ensure large Δ_{BL} even at low supply voltages. During, write '1' operation, the BL voltage should be maintained at high level. To ensure this, the simulations are carried out for bitline voltage BL at $V_{DD} = 1.1$ V and 0.9 V under 3σ global process variations in PG [9] (bitline leakage uncompensated) and proposed (bitline leakage compensated) designs and are shown in Fig. 4. From the results it can be noted that the BL voltage drops by 26.59% at $V_{DD} = 1.1$ V (Fig. 4(a)) and 27.06% at $V_{DD} = 0.9$ V (Fig. 4(b)) in the PG [9] design. However, its value is maintained almost equal to V_{DD} independent of the supply voltage level in the proposed design (Fig. 4(c) and Fig. 4(d)). This occurs, due to the use of leakage-compensation mechanism in the proposed design whereas it is not possible in case of existing uncompensated designs due to the flow of high magnitude bitline leakage currents.

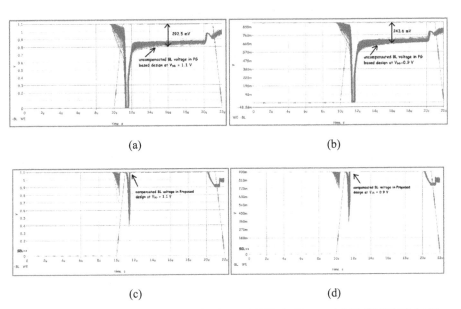

(a)   (b)

(c)   (d)

Fig. 4. Bitline voltage during write operation in (a) PG [9] (at $V_{DD} = 1.1$ V) (b) PG [9] (at $V_{DD} = 0.9$ V) (c) Proposed (at $V_{DD} = 1.1$ V) (d) Proposed (at $V_{DD} = 0.9$ V) designs

5 Simulation and Discussion

In this section, the performance parameters T_{WD} (write delay), P_W (write power consumption), E_W (energy consumption per switching activity) and Δ_{BL} (differential bitline voltage) are captured for proposed and the existing designs (discussed in Sect. 3) at 32 nm technology node. All the simulations are performed using SYMICA SPICE simulation tool. The pMOS and nMOS transistors have the threshold voltage (V_{th}) as -0.452 V and 0.483 V respectively. The C_{BL} and C_{BLB} of bitlines is assumed to be 80 fF. The robustness of the design is verified by performing simulations at different supplies (1.3 V down to 0.9 V), corners (SS, SF, TT, FS, FF) and temperatures (125 °C down to $-$40 °C). To capture the effect of diverse conditions on the designs, simulations that are more extensive in nature are performed under frequency variations and PVT-variations with 3σ global process variations. For fair comparison, the corresponding transistors having same aspect ratio are used.

Table 1 summarizes the results at 1.1 V, TT corner, 27 °C and displays the best values in bold font. The results indicate that the proposed and NG [12] designs perform the fastest write operation and provides 9.9%, 2.9% and 4.9% improvement in T_{WD} over PG [9], AG [11] and TG [11] designs respectively. However, NG [12] design consumes the highest P_W and E_W compared to proposed and other existing designs. It is worth mentioning that the proposed design provides the fastest write and consumes 26.75% less P_W and 26.03% less E_W than NG [12] design. The proposed design is thus low power and more energy efficient than NG [12] design. In addition, the proposed design provides up to 29.13% higher Δ_{BL} than existing designs.

Table 1. Write Mode Simulation Results at 1.1 V, TT, and 27 °C

Write driver	Parameter			
	T_{WD} (ns)	P_W (nW)	E_W (pJ)	Δ_{BL}(mV)
PG [9]	1.11	**4790.51**	**2.65**	852.35
AG [11]	1.04	7141.67	3.71	851.62
TG [11]	1.06	8995.58	4.78	989.73
NG [12]	1.01	10865.87	5.47	1099.69
Proposed	**1.01**	8572.3	4.34	**1099.72**
% age improvement	**up to 9.9%**	**up to 26.75%**	**up to 26.03%**	**up to 29.13%**

The results from comparative analysis of all the designs is tabulated in Table 2. The results show that due to use of leakage-compensation circuitry, stacking effect and reduction of transistors in the path of discharging bitlines, the proposed write driver design shows improved write delay performance at lower P_W and E_W compared to existing designs.

Table 2. Summary Comparison of Performance among Various Existing Write Driver Designs

Design	Transistor count in bitline discharge path	Leakage compensation mechanism	Comparative analysis
AG [11]	1	No	Low P_W, Moderate T_{WD}
PG [9]	2	No	Least P_W, Highest T_{WD}
TG [11]	2	No	High P_W, Moderate T_{WD}
NG [12]	1	Yes	Highest P_W, Low T_{WD}
Proposed	1	Yes	Less P_W and E_W than NG [12] and TG [11], Least T_{WD} among all

5.1 Process Corner based Variations

Figure 5 depicts the impact of variations on performance parameters due to fabrication process at a supply voltage of 1.1 V and temperature of 27 °C. The results (Fig. 5(a)) show that the write delay, T_{WD}, is not a strong function of process variations at non-skewed process corners, however, the parameter varies significantly at skewed corners 'SF' and 'FS'. The reason for this is that at process corner 'SF', the current capability of pMOS transistors is much higher than that of nMOS transistors resulting in a slow write operation. The reverse thing occurs at opposite corner. However, the proposed and NG [12] designs outdo all the other designs regardless of process corners and achieve up to 10.5% improvement in write delay over other designs. It is also noted that the write power consumption P_W (Fig. 5(b)) shows a strong dependence on process corners with the best performance at 'SS' corner and worst performance at 'FF' corner due to reduced driving strength of transistors at 'SS' corner and increased strength at 'FF' corner respectively. However, the proposed design consumes up to 22.4% less P_W than NG [12] and TG [11] designs due to stacking of transistors in core structure that reduces the leakages in proposed design [6]. It is also revealed in Fig. 5(c) that energy consumption of the circuit E_W depends upon the driving capabilities of transistors and shows worst and best values at 'FF' and 'SS' corners respectively. The proposed design consumes 21.8% less E_W than NG [12] and TG [11] designs across the process corners.

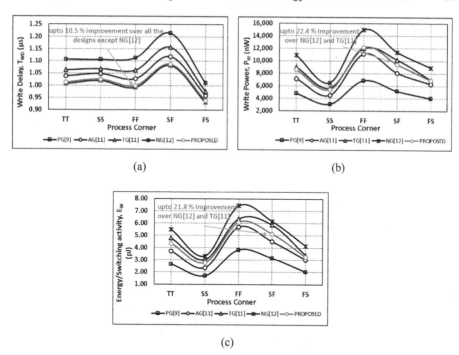

Fig. 5. Process corner based variations on (a) T_{WD} (b) P_W (c) E_W

5.2 Supply Voltage Based Variations

Figure 6 elucidates the influence of variations in supply voltage on different performance parameters at a temperature of 27 °C and process corner TT. The analysis reveals that as the supply voltage increases from 0.9 V to 1.3 V, the strength of transistors also enhances and results in faster write operation with low T_{WD} and higher P_W and E_W values. However, the proposed design shows impeccable performance with up to 9.5% improvement in T_{WD} (Fig. 6(a)) over other designs. In addition, the proposed design shows up to 25.8% improvement in P_W (Fig. 6(b)) and 29.5% improvement in E_W (Fig. 6(c)) over NG [12] and TG [11] designs.

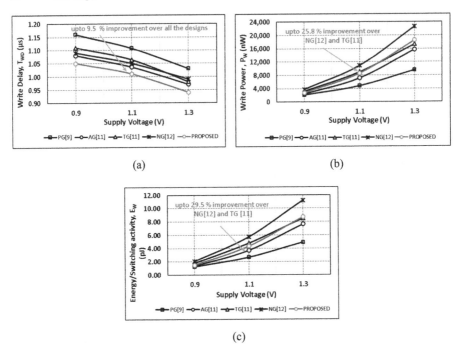

Fig. 6. Supply voltage based variations on (a) T_{WD} (b) P_W (c) E_W

5.3 Temperature Based Variations

Figure 7 illustrates the outcome of variations in temperature on the parameters of all designs at a supply voltage of 1.1 V and process corner TT. As the temperature reduces from 125 °C to −40 °C, the transistors become slower resulting in dilatory write operation, however, the proposed design executes the fastest write and achieves up to 12.7% enhancement in T_{WD} (Fig. 7(a)) over other designs. The power and energy consumption values also show similar trend wherein the proposed design shows up to 21.1% improvement in P_W (Fig. 7(b)) and 24.1% improvement in E_W (Fig. 7(c)) over NG [12] and TG [11] designs.

5.4 PVT-variations

The write performance of all designs vary under PVT-variations. The PVT-variations are reflected in terms of changes in the threshold voltage of transistors. A 10% variation in V_{th} of nMOS and pMOS transistors is considered to capture the effect of PVT-variations on T_{WD} of the designs.

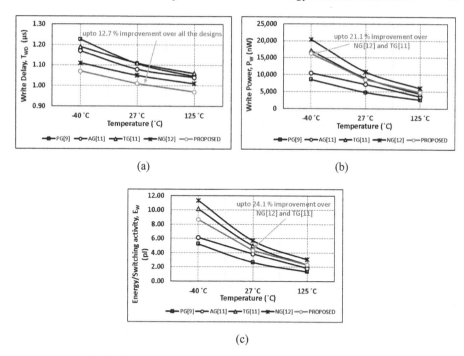

Fig. 7. Temperature based variations on (a) T_{WD} (b) P_W (c) E_W

The distribution of T_{WD} values for all designs at $V_{DD} = 1.1$ V under 3σ global process variations is plotted in Fig. 8. The analysis reveals that the proposed design executes the fastest write under PVT-variations, in addition to reduced deviation in values around the mean value. It is worth mentioning that the proposed design shows 8.84%, 2.11% and 4.77%, reduction in mean value of T_{WD} compared to PG [9], AG [11] and TG [11] write driver designs respectively whereas the performance remains comparable to NG [12] design. In addition, the proposed design shows 59.66%, 26.81%, 26.53% and 11.81% reduced deviation in T_{WD} values compared to PG [9], AG [11], TG [11] and NG [12] write driver designs respectively.

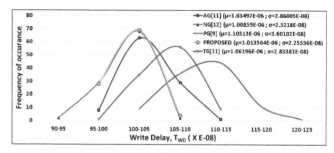

Fig. 8. Distribution of T_{WD} of all the designs at $V_{DD} = 1.1$ V under 3σ global process variations

The distribution of Δ_{BL} values during write '1' operation when WE is pulled high in the write driver, for PG [9] (leakage uncompensated) and proposed (leakage compensated) designs at $V_{DD} = 1.1$ V and $V_{DD} = 0.9$ V under 3σ global process variations is plotted in Fig. 9. It can be verified from the results that the Δ_{BL} that should remain equal to V_{DD} during write '1' operation, reduces to 852.35 mV at $V_{DD} = 1.1$ V (Fig. 9(a)) and 693.34 mV at $V_{DD} = 0.9$ V (Fig. 9(b)) in the PG [9] design. However, in proposed design it remains at 1099.70 mV at $V_{DD} = 1.1$ V and 899.80 mV at $V_{DD} = 0.9$ V showing 29.01% and 29.78% improvement in Δ_{BL} with 98.16% and 99.12% reduced deviation respectively from their mean value.

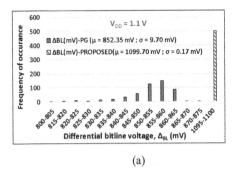 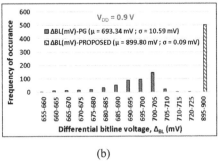

(a)   (b)

Fig. 9. Distribution of Δ_{BL} in PG [9] and proposed designs during write '1' operation at (a) V_{DD} = 1.1 V (b) $V_{DD} = 0.9$ V under 3σ global process variations

5.5 Frequency Based Variations

The results of variation in clock frequency on the performance parameters at a supply voltage of 1.1 V, process corner TT and a temperature 27 °C is illustrated in Fig. 10. From the results, few important observations can be made. First, it can be verified that the performance of all the designs remain almost independent of frequency. Second, the proposed design shows up to 8.8% in T_{WD} (Fig. 10(a)) over all except NG [12] design. In addition, it shows up to 33.7% and 33.5% improvement in P_W (Fig. 10(b)) and E_W (Fig. 10(c)) over NG [12] and TG [11] designs supporting the claim that the proposed design offers unparalleled performance not provided by existing designs.

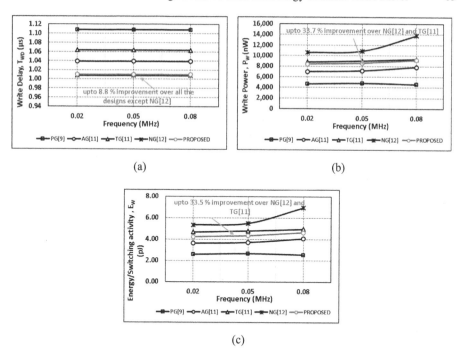

Fig. 10. Frequency based variations on (a) T_{WD} (b) P_W (c) E_W

6 Conclusion

In this paper, a novel design for a write driver with faster writing, and low write power and reduced energy consumption for SRAM is presented. The use of a reduced number of transistors in the discharge paths of bitlines, along with a unique leakage-compensation control mechanism and a stacking effect, results in a faster write operation while maintaining low power and energy consumption. The design achieves up to a 10.5%, 22.4% and 21.8% improvement in delay, power consumption and energy consumption per switching activity under process corner based variations. Under supply voltage based variations, a 9.5%, 25.8% and 29.5% improvement is achieved in the same parameters. Additionally, the proposed design provides a 12.7%, 21.1% and 24.1% improvement in the same parameters under temperature based variations. To demonstrate the impeccable performance of the proposed design, its performance is also evaluated under PVT-variations with 3σ global process variations. The results indicate that the proposed design outperforms all the existing designs and achieves the fastest write operation regardless of supply voltage, process corner and temperature, with up to 8.84% faster operation. Due to the use of leakage-compensation mechanism, the proposed design exhibits a 29.01% higher differential bitline voltage with a 98.16% reduced deviation compared to un-compensated designs at 1.1 V. Furthermore, the variation in clock frequency has no impact on the impeccable performance of the proposed design, which shows improvements of up to 8.8%, 33.7% and 33.5% in delay, power consumption and energy consumption per switching activity over other designs. Thus, the proposed design proves to be a superior alternative to pass-gate and AND-gate based designs for high-speed applications due to its low write delay. Additionally, the proposed design is also appropriate for applications such as wireless sensor networks, portable devices, biomedical implants etc., due to its high energy efficiency and low write power in comparison to NOR-gate and transmission-gate based designs.

References

1. Abbasian, E., Sofimowloodi, S.: Energy-efficient single-ended Read/Write 10T near-threshold SRAM. IEEE Trans. Circuits Syst. I Regul. Pap. **70**(5), 2037–2047 (2023). https://doi.org/10.1109/TCSI.2023.3247807
2. Gupta, M., et al.: A data-independent 9T SRAM cell with enhanced ION/IOFF ratio and RBL voltage swing in near threshold and sub-threshold region. Int. J. Circuit Theory Appl. **49**, 953–969 (2021). https://doi.org/10.1002/cta.2951
3. Yan, A., et al.: Novel speed-and-power-optimized SRAM cell designs with enhanced self-recoverability from single- and double-node upsets. IEEE Trans. Circuits Syst. I Regul. Pap. **67**(12), 4684–4695 (2020). https://doi.org/10.1109/TCSI.2020.3018328
4. Rajaei, R., et al.: Single event multiple upset-tolerant SRAM cell designs for nano-scale CMOS technology. Turkish J. Elect. Eng. Comput. Sci. **25**(1), 1035–1047 (2017). https://doi.org/10.3906/elk-1502-124
5. Gupta, M., et al.: A novel PVT-variation-tolerant Schmitt-trigger-based 12T SRAM cell with improved write ability and high ION/IOFF ratio in sub-threshold region. Int. J. Circuit Theory Appl. **49**(11), 3789–3810 (2021). https://doi.org/10.1002/cta.3134
6. Gupta, M., et al.: Comparative analysis of the design techniques for low leakage SRAMs at 32 nm. J. Microprocess. Microsyst. **85**, 1–19 (2021). https://doi.org/10.1016/j.micpro.2021.104281
7. Wu, C.W., et al.: A configurable 2-in-1 SRAM compiler with constant-negative-level write driver for low Vmin in 16 nm Fin-FET CMOS. In: IEEE Asian Solid-State Circuits Conference, pp. 145–148 (2014). https://doi.org/10.1109/ASSCC.2014.7008881
8. Andre, T.W., et al.: A 4-Mb 0.18-m 1T1MTJ toggle MRAM with balanced three input sensing scheme and locally mirrored unidirectional write drivers. IEEE J. Solid-State Circuits **40**(1), 301–308 (2005). https://doi.org/10.1109/JSSC.2004.837962
9. Sharma, P., et al.: A low power subthreshold Schmitt Trigger based 12T SRAM bit cell with process-variation-tolerant write-ability. Microelectron. J. **97**, 1–13 (2020). https://doi.org/10.1016/j.mejo.2020.104703
10. Gupta, S., et al.: Low-power near-threshold 10T SRAM bit cells with enhanced data-independent read port leakage for array augmentation in 32-nm CMOS. IEEE Trans. Circuits Syst. I Regul. Pap. **66**(3), 978–988 (2019). https://doi.org/10.1109/TCSI.2018.2876785
11. Singh, J., et al.: Robust SRAM Designs and Analysis, 1st edn. Springer, New York (2013). https://doi.org/10.1007/978-1-4614-0818-5
12. Ney, A., et al.: A design-for-diagnosis technique for SRAM write drivers. In: Design, Automation and Test in Europe, Munich, Germany, pp. 1480–1485 (2008). https://doi.org/10.1109/DATE.2008.4484883
13. Sharma, P., Hashmi, M.S.: A novel design of a dual functionality Read-Write driver for SRAM. In: IEEE International SOC Conference, pp. 280–285 (2016). https://doi.org/10.1109/SOCC.2016.7905487

Review of Synergistic Integration of Microstrip Patch Antennas in Biomedical and Artificial Intelligence Domains

Bimal Raj Dutta[1]([✉]) and Balaka Biswas[2]

[1] ECE Department, Chandigarh University, Mohali, India
brajdutta@gmail.com
[2] Mechatronics Department, Chandigarh University, Mohali, India

Abstract. Biomedical imaging with microstrip patch antennas has indeed shown encouraging outcomes in different platforms, including protein characterization and cancer detection. Non-ionizing radiation-based techniques of biomedical imaging, such as ultrasonic and microwave imaging, are being investigated for the early diagnosis of skin cancer, which is one of the most prevalent forms of cancer due to its exposure to sunlight. Ultrasonic imaging, which creates images of the inner structures of the body using sound waves, is a widely used medical application for detecting and diagnosing skin tumors. It can also help to identify abnormal tissue characteristics, such as changes in tissue density, which may indicate the presence of a tumor. It is particularly useful in distinguishing between solid masses and fluid-filled cysts. RFID-based sensors in biomedical imaging offer several advantages that make them suitable for structural health monitoring (SHM) applications. They are passive devices that can operate wirelessly. This passive nature eliminates the need for frequent battery replacements and reduces maintenance efforts in large-scale infrastructures. Additionally, the wireless operation allows for remote sensing and monitoring, enhancing convenience and accessibility. Microstrip patch antennas have been significantly used for different purposes, such as wireless communication within medical devices, wearable health monitoring systems, and biomedical imaging.

Keywords: Ultrawide Bandwidth · SHM · Radio frequency identification · Redesigned sensors · Microstrip patch antenna

1 Introduction

The Microwave Technology has been growing so fast in Bio-medical and Satellite Communication which bring on the significant increase in several aeras such as cross check, protein characterization, pharmaceutical, cancer detection applying non-ionizing radiation, and satellite communications integrated through solar cells. The Quality control is an essential aspect of the manufacturing process of any product, including pharmaceuticals, electronics, and other industries [1, 2]. Quality control ensures that products meet the desired quality standards, and all manufacturing processes follow a defined set

R. C. Bansal et al. (Eds.): ACTET 2023, CCIS 2000, pp. 65–81, 2024.
https://doi.org/10.1007/978-3-031-54162-9_5

of protocols. Protein characterization involves identifying and analyzing the structure, function, and interactions of proteins. This information is critical in understanding the role of proteins in biological processes and diseases. Pharmaceuticals are compounds designed to treat, cure, or prevent diseases. Advancement of pharmaceuticals comprise of various steps, containing drug discovery, pre-clinical development, clinical trials, and regulatory approval. Non-ionizing radiation, such as visible light, infrared radiation, and radio waves, can be geared toward cancer detection. Imaging techniques like optical coherence tomography (OCT), diffuse optical tomography (DOT), and magnetic resonance imaging (MRI) are examples of non-ionizing radiation-based imaging techniques used for cancer detection. Satellite communications are used for various applications, including weather forecasting, navigation, and communication. The use of solar cells in satellite communication systems is becoming increasingly popular as solar cells provide authentic and acceptable origin of strength for satellites. Microstrip patch antenna is a type of antenna that consists of a flat metal patch, typically made of copper or other conductive material, affixed on a skinny dielectric substrate, that one is placed above a ground plane. The metal patch is usually a few millimeters in size and has a specific shape, like rectangular, circular, triangular, conversely further forms. The patch is normally supplied through a coaxial cable or further transmission line, which is joined to a fine feed point on the patch. Microstrip patch antennas are widely used in various uses, containing mobile devices, wireless communication systems, satellite communication systems, and radar systems, owing to their compact size, low profile, low cost, and smooth merger to microwave tracks. For many wireless communication approaches Microstrip patch antennas are a favored option as it has several benefits such as compact size, low profile, negligible cost, and ease of integration with microwave integrated circuits (MIC/MMIC). They are also compatible one and the other symmetrical and unsymmetrical areas, making them suitable for a wide range of applications.

The rectangular, square, triangular, and circular patch shapes are normally applied forms for microstrip patch antennas. Skin cancer is a kind of disease which grows inside the cells of the skin. It occurs when skin cells are damaged, and their DNA mutates, causing them to grow and divide uncontrollably, leading to the formation of a mass or tumor. X-rays, MRI, and ultrasound are some of the common imaging techniques used for medical diagnosis. However, ultra-wideband technology is gaining popularity in recent times as it offers high-resolution imaging and can differentiate between healthy and unhealthy tissues more accurately. Ultra-wideband technology uses short pulses of electromagnetic waves that penetrate the skin and provide detailed images of the underlying tissue. This technology is non-invasive, safe, and can be used for early detection of skin cancer. It can detect changes in skin tissue at a very early stage, even before they become visible to the naked eye or with other imaging techniques. Ultra-wideband technology can also be used for monitoring the progression of cancer and evaluating the effectiveness of treatment. It can provide real-time images of the cancerous tissue, allowing doctors to track the changes in the tumor and adjust the treatment accordingly. Ultra-wideband technology has immense potential at the level of medical imaging, especially for the primitive diagnosis and monitoring about skin cancer. It offers a safe and non-invasive alternative to traditional imaging techniques and can help save lives by enabling timely and accurate diagnosis. The most intriguing use of ultrawide band technology in biomedicine is to distinguish between healthy and sick tissues, like in the case of skin and chest cancer diagnosis [3–5].

The UWB technology displays good results which gives extensive bandwidth in with low power [6] and due to its wide bandwidth and low power consumption, UWB technology produces positive benefits. Microstrip patch antenna plays an important role in bio medical applications as now a days microstrip patch antenna is becoming very popular and important for monitoring of health. The main antennas that are being used these days are BWCS and RFID sensors. Battery powered sensors have applications of current wireless application sensors but the sensors are more costly than the normal regular sensors and it limits the count of detail in the particular data of action [7]. Because battery-powered sensors have a short lifespan, disposing of billions of batteries poses a long-term ecological danger [8].

Sensors may not need to be highly sophisticated or accurate due to their intended widespread use, but all should meet demands for economical and reasonable stability in the interest for positioned with greater resolution compared to actively accurate wireless sensors. Designing "smart dust motes," or autonomously monitoring, ubiquitous computing, and communication systems that are compact enough to simply distributed in the surroundings," is the ultimate goal [9]. This inspires the evolution of economical, wireless, and passive sensors considering big information including extensive infrastructure utilizations.

Radio frequency technology (RFID) is a technology which can be utilized to work on low-cost sensors, wireless sensors, and it is sensing friendly as well. The RFID has seen rapid growth in the last few years as it is used for identification and enabling the recognition due to its Unique identification. Without the use of extra electronics or sensors, cognate filtering for the actual waves linked to reader-level conversation may make it possible to obtain substantially more data about the target. Microstrip patch antenna is used in artificial intelligence as well because they play a vital role in the overall communication and connectivity aspects of AI domain (Fig. 1).

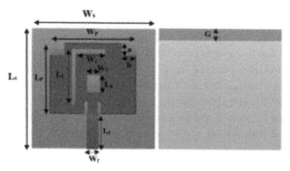

Fig. 1. Geometry of proposed Antenna Front view, Back view [36]

2 Literature Review

2.1 Microstrip Antenna in Bio-Medical

A microstrip patch antenna is kind of antenna which comprise of a conducting patch form on top of a dielectric substrate, with a ground plane on the opposite side. This configuration allows that antenna to be relatively small and lightweight, making it suitable for various applications, including biomedical applications. In the field of biomedical engineering, microstrip patch antennas have been utilized for different purposes, such as wireless communication within medical devices, wearable health monitoring systems, and biomedical imaging.

The applications of Micro-strip patch antenna are:

- Wireless Biomedical Implants: Microstrip patch antennas can be integrated into biomedical implants, such as pacemakers or neurostimulators, to enable wireless communication. These antennas allow data transmission between the implant and an external device, such as a programmer or monitoring system, without the need for physical connections.
- Biomedical Imaging Systems: Microstrip patch antennas find applications in various imaging techniques, including microwave imaging (magnetic resonance imaging). In microwave imaging, these antennas help transmit and receive microwave signals for generating detailed images of internal body structures. In MRI, microstrip patch antennas are used as RF coils to transmit and receive radiofrequency signals during the imaging process.
- Review of research [10] states that a Microstrip patch antenna of Z slot has been implanted for skin cancer detection by analyzing specific absorption rate (SAR) value. The antenna has used RT/Duroid 5880 substrate of 3.4 relative permittivity and operated at 6 GHz. This has resulted reduce exposure of skin radiation and detection of Cancer from comparison of parameters (Like voltage standing wave ratio (VSWR), S11, (return loss), efficiency and gain between malignent cells and healthy cells.
- Wearable Health Monitoring Systems: Microstrip patch antennas are utilized in wearable devices for continuous health monitoring. These antennas enable the wireless transmission of physiological data, such as heart rate, body temperature, or ECG signals, from wearable sensors to a central monitoring unit or a smartphone application. The paper [11] has researched on body wearable patch antenna designing. The Patch antenna for 2.45 GHz operating frequency, has been designed for Gain enhancement by replacing the cotton substrate material with textile substrate. Antenna with inset feeding has been simulated for gain measurement by changing the parameters (length, width, operating frequency and dielectric constant) for both type of substrates. it has gain of 5.89 dB with leather textile substrate better than 5.75 dB for cotton textile substrate.
- Body Area Networks (BANs): Microstrip patch antennas play a crucial role in establishing wireless communication within body area networks. In BANs, multiple wearable or implantable devices equipped with microstrip patch antennas form a network to exchange data and facilitate real-time monitoring of vital signs and other health-related parameters. Sometimes the BAN (Body Area Networks) is present consists of instruments inside the human body.

- The paper [12] has presented a review study on different parameters of designing a patch antenna for Body Area Network (BAN). The Handy and useful embedded devices have made three ways of change in electromagnetic radiations in BAN applications. Implantation of Sensors in human body for analysis of performance is one-way, while observing the history of elder one's data is the second way. Use of MRI, CT-Scan, endoscopic test etc. methods of testing is the third way in BAN.

- Telemedicine and Remote Patient Monitoring: Microstrip patch antennas are employed in telemedicine applications, where remote patient monitoring is essential. By integrating these antennas into wearable devices or home monitoring systems, healthcare providers can remotely monitor patients' health conditions and receive real-time data for analysis and diagnosis. an issue can be evaded by using wearable antennas which can get completely integrated onto clothes and use it for remotely transmitting/receiving the sensor data without affecting the elderly's regular habits.

- The paper [13] has explained the obstructions for manufacturing of highly efficient wearable patch antenna. The patch has been manufactured with use of FR4 substrate ($\epsilon r = 4.3$, and loss tangent $\delta = 0.025$) at operating frequency of 2.3 GHz and Denim material substrate (relative permittivity $\epsilon r = 1.67$, and the loss tangent $\tan \delta = 0.085$) for operating frequency 2.66 GHz. The patch antenna has shown an improved parameters for real conditions. Microwave Hyperthermia Therapy: Microstrip patch antennas are used in hyperthermia therapy, a treatment method that involves heating specific body tissues to destroy cancer cells or treat other medical conditions. These antennas deliver controlled microwave energy to the targeted tissues, raising their temperature and causing localized cell damage.

- The reviewed paper [14] has fabricated Archimedean spiral micro strip antenna (ASMPA) on FR-4 substrate. The patch has improved parameters (gain of 3.1 dB, Voltage Standing Wave Ratio < 2, Specific Absorption Ratio and temperature rise over the infected affect area of bio mimic 8 W/Kg and 42 °C). It is effective in different-layered (skin, muscle and fat) human mimic.

- Wireless Capsule Endoscopy: Microstrip patch antennas are integrated into wireless capsule endoscopy devices. These antennas enable the transmission of high-resolution images and videos captured by the endoscope as it passes through the digestive tract. This allows for non-invasive visualization and diagnosis of gastrointestinal disorders (Fig. 2).

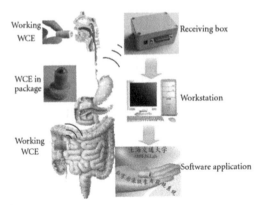

Fig. 2. Image of Wireless Capsule Endoscopy

- The paper [15–17] has researched a device for the imaging process of the digestive system. Patch antenna being the part of endoscopy capsule designed device has used fractal geometry for ultra-wideband technology (UWB). It has improved image processing due to improved parameters (return loss −25.1 dB at 5.45 GHz, VSWR 1.13 and Omni-directional radiation patterns).

These are just a few examples of how microstrip patch antennas are employed in biomedical applications. The versatility, compactness, and compatibility with modern wireless technologies make them valuable components in the development of advanced biomedical devices and systems (Figs. 3, 4 and 5).

Elangovan et al. [18] designed a hexagonal shaped patch antenna with meandering for biomedical applications. The biomedical applications require low latency and high bandwidth to transmit patient information which requires multi band transmission. With this hexagonal shaped meandering antenna provides greater bandwidth and improved gain characteristic.

2.2 Radio Frequency Identification (RFID) Technology Used in Bio-Medical

RFID (Radio Frequency Identification) technology is commonly practiced over various industries, including the biomedical field, for tracking, identification, and data retrieval purposes. Due to economical, cordless nature, and "careful-beneficial" features, RFID (radio frequency identification) may serve an important part [19]. Microstrip patch antennas can be integrated into RFID systems to enable wireless communication and enhance the performance of RFID-based biomedical applications. Here's how RFID and microstrip patch antennas are used in biomedical contexts:

Medical Equipment and Asset Tracking: RFID tags attached to medical equipment, such as surgical instruments, can be tracked using RFID readers deployed throughout a healthcare facility. Microstrip patch antennas can be utilized in RFID readers to enhance the read range and sensitivity of the system, ensuring accurate and efficient tracking of medical assets. Implantable devices like pacemakers have become more effective in the health care system nowadays.

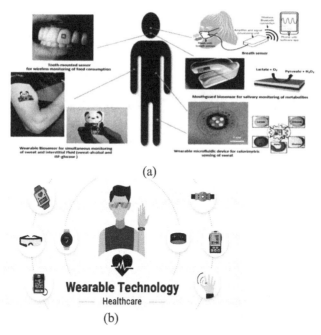

(a)

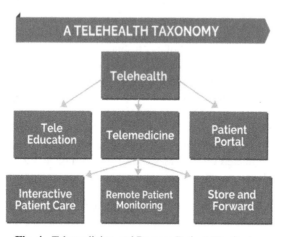

(b)

Fig. 3. Health monitoring devices that can be worn wearable devices.

Fig. 4. Telemedicine and Remote Patient Monitoring

The paper [8] has reviewed different patch antenna for bio- implantation applications. These patch antennae have received signal from sensors and radiates negative gain due to fluids of human body. Different biomedical applications (glucose level monitoring, deep brain stimulation, wireless endoscopy, laparoscopy, implementation of pacemaker, temperature and blood pressure monitor) have experienced improved gain and radiation from these Miniaturized Patch antennae.

Fig. 5. Recent microstrip antenna for Biomedical application [18]

Patient Identification and Monitoring: RFID wristbands or tags can be used to identify and track patients within a healthcare setting. These tags can store patient information and enable healthcare providers to access relevant data quickly. Microstrip patch antennas integrated into RFID readers facilitate reliable and long-range communication with patient tags, allowing for seamless identification and monitoring.

The paper [20] has designed a patch antenna for analyzing the electrolyte (NaCl) level from the sweat of human skin. The designed antenna has applied different dielectric substrates from 1.0 F/m–2.0 F/m values. It has improved parameters (frequency range of 0.5 GHz–3.5 GHz, operating frequency 1.57 GHz) for applied non-invasive method. The parameters (resonant frequency and reflection magnitude) of Patch antenna have been changing due to different level of electrolyte.

Pharmaceutical Supply Chain Management: RFID tags can be affixed to medication packages or vials to monitor and track their movement through the supply chain. Microstrip patch antennas in RFID readers help capture the data stored on the tags, such as product information, expiration dates, and batch numbers, enabling efficient inventory management and reducing the risk of counterfeit or expired drugs. A square slot patch antenna for wireless communication has been designed in the paper [21]. This Patch antenna has been fabricated on FR4 lossy substrate with dielectric constant of 4.3 and operating at 3.5 GHz frequency. It has improved performance with VSWR less than 1.2 value.

Implantable Medical Devices: RFID technology combined with microstrip patch antennas can be utilized in implantable medical devices for various purposes. For example, RFID tags embedded in pacemakers or implantable drug delivery systems can store patient-specific information or medication dosing details. Microstrip patch antennas in external RFID readers allow healthcare professionals to wirelessly access and update the information stored in the implantable devices.

Laboratory Sample Tracking: RFID tags attached to laboratory samples, such as blood vials or tissue specimens, can help track their location and status during processing and storage. Microstrip patch antennas in RFID readers ensure reliable and accurate scanning of the tags, streamlining sample management, and minimizing errors in the laboratory workflow.

The paper [22] has a Z slot Microstrip patch antenna implantation for skin cancer detection using specific absorption rate (SAR) value. The antenna with RT/Duroid 5880 substrate of 3.4 relative permittivity has operated at 6 GHz. Patch antenna has reduced exposure of skin radiation and detection of Cancer due to comparison of parameters (gain, voltage standing wave ratio (VSWR), and return loss) between cancer cells and healthy cells.

Biomedical Research and Animal Tracking: RFID tags can be used to track research subjects or laboratory animals in biomedical studies. Microstrip patch antennas integrated into RFID readers facilitate the identification and monitoring of individual animals within a facility, enabling researchers to collect data on their behavior, health, and response to treatments. In electromagnetic spectrum terahertz region is sandwich between the microwave and IR region. The low photon energy-based terahertz waves are used for cancer diagnosis in this research [22]. Cancer affected cells are identified by these waves due to observation of blood in the tissues. The metamaterials-based antenna has been designed for terahertz spectroscopy techniques. The antenna parameters have also been observed for these waves' transmission in the affected tissues.

In these applications, microstrip patch antennas are utilized in RFID readers to enhance the communication range, sensitivity, and accuracy of RFID systems. The design and optimization of the antenna are crucial to ensure reliable wireless communication and maximize the efficiency of the RFID-based biomedical applications. The phrase "antenna sensor" refers to one form of sensor used in this context that makes use of antennae to "sense" objects [23].

Antenna sensors put on referred surfaces operate on a similar concept to vibrated eddy current nondestructive testing (NDT) [24], whose impart damage as well as extent of penetration are equivalent to resonance frequency. The spatial clarity can be continually improved by raising the operating frequency by a matching reduction in wavelengths [25] and antenna size.

The communicating dimension between an RFID level and reader communicator in the moderate frequency (LF) or higher frequency (HF) bandwidth is somewhat restricted as a result of magnetic resonance couplings (MRC), as the in the context of wireless power transfer (WPT) [26]. UHF and ultra-wide band (UWB) antennas probably employed to improve communications because of electromagnetic (EM) interaction [27] (Fig. 6).

Internet of Things (IoT) of the tomorrow are going to be made up of composite linked gadgets will additionally expand the boundaries for globe owing to both real and virtual elements [28]. Internal information is such as seamless access for Cloud Computing system, while middleware is built such as possible incorporation for heterogeneity IoT sensor network [29].

2.3 Microstrip Patch Antenna in Artificial Intelligence

In the context of artificial intelligence (AI), a microstrip patch antenna refers to kind of antenna which is used for wireless communication and connectivity within AI systems. A microstrip antenna is a compact and planar antenna design which contains metallic patch placed over dielectric substrate, typically thin and low-loss material. The microstrip patch antenna is called "microstrip" because it operates using the principle of microstrip

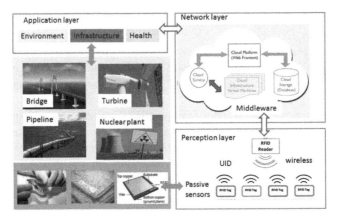

Fig. 6. Resigned Radio Frequency Sensor

transmission line, where the metallic patch acts as a radiating element, and the dielectric substrate acts as a transmission line. The patch is typically a rectangular or circular shape and is printed on top of the dielectric substrate. Bottom side of the substrate is usually ground plane, which provides the necessary reference for the antenna's operation. In AI applications, microstrip patch antennas are employed to establish wireless communication and connectivity between various AI-enabled devices and components. They enable the transfer of data, information, and control signals wirelessly, facilitating the interaction and coordination of AI systems. Microstrip patch antennas are utilized in AI systems to enable wireless communication, data transmission, and connectivity between AI devices and components. They play a vital role in establishing the wireless linkages that facilitate the operation and coordination of AI systems in diverse applications.

2.4 Advantages of Microstrip Patch Antenna in Artificial Intelligence

- Compact Size: Microstrip patch antennas are small in size and have a low profile that is suitable for integration into small and portable AI devices, wearable devices, or embedded systems.
- Low Cost: Microstrip patch antennas are relatively low cost to manufacture compared to other antenna designs, making them cost-effective for mass production and deployment in AI systems.
- Ease of Integration: Microstrip patch antennas can be easily integrated into AI devices and systems due to their planar and thin structure. They can be printed on flexible or rigid substrates, allowing for versatile integration options.
- Broadband and Multiband Operation: Microstrip patch antennas can be designed to operate over a wide range of frequencies or support multiple frequency bands, enabling compatibility with various wireless communication standards and protocols.
- Directional or Omni-directional Radiation Patterns: Subjected to the specific design, microstrip patch antennas can be engineered to have directional radiation patterns for focused communication or omni-directional patterns for broader coverage.

2.5 Application of Microstrip Patch Antenna in Artificial Intelligence

Microstrip patch antennas find several applications in artificial intelligence (AI) systems. Here are some specific applications where microstrip patch antennas are utilized in the context of AI:

Wireless Sensor Networks: Microstrip patch antennas can be employed in AI-driven wireless sensor networks. They enable wireless communication between AI-powered sensors, allowing data to be collected, transmitted, and analyzed for various applications such as environmental monitoring, smart agriculture, or industrial automation.

Robotics and Autonomous Systems: Microstrip patch antennas are used in AI-powered robots and autonomous systems for wireless communication. They facilitate the exchange of data, commands, and control signals between different robotic components or between robots and their control systems, enabling coordinated actions and intelligent decision-making. To examine the structure strain wirelessly a new passive detection technique called strain sensing technology consists of microstrip patch has developed for industrial application purposes.

The paper [30] has designed patch antenna-based strain sensor. It has used frequency doubling sensor with patch antenna for both transmitter and receiver sections. Both sections are connected through frequency multiplier circuit. It has a direct relation between antenna resonant frequency and strain of the sensor. It has improved the wireless detection range.

Edge Computing and AI at the Edge: Microstrip patch antennas play a role in AI systems that leverage edge computing. They provide wireless connectivity between edge devices and AI processing units, enabling distributed data processing and analysis at the edge of the network. This reduces latency, optimizes bandwidth usage, and enhances real-time decision-making capabilities.

The paper [31] has explained about the fractal pattern diamond shape patch antenna design. On substrate FR-4(permittivity 4.4), the designed patch for different wireless applications((LTE), point to multi-point and ultra-wide band) has controlled parameters (Return Loss (RL) of -23.01dB and the Voltage Standing Wave Ratio (VSWR) of 1.64) for various operating frequency ranges (3.8, 5.6, 8.2 GHz). It is mainly applicable for 5G communication system.

AI-Enabled Wearable Devices: Microstrip patch antennas can be integrated into wearable devices with AI capabilities, such as smartwatches, fitness trackers, or healthcare monitoring devices. These antennas enable wireless connectivity, allowing wearable devices to communicate with other devices, cloud-based AI platforms, or smartphone applications for data transfer, analysis, and interaction.

Internet of Things (IoT) and AI: Microstrip patch antennas are used in AI-enabled IoT systems. They provide wireless connectivity for IoT devices, enabling seamless communication between devices and the AI infrastructure. This facilitates data collection, analysis, and control in AI-driven IoT functions, like smart homes, smart cities, or industrial IoT.

Intelligent Transportation Systems: Microstrip patch antennas play a crucial role in AI applications for intelligent transportation systems. They enable wireless communication between vehicles, infrastructure, and AI platforms for applications like vehicle-to-vehicle (V2V) and vehicle-to-infrastructure (V2I) communication, Self-governing driving, and traffic management.

Surveillance and Security Systems: Microstrip patch antennas are utilized in AI-powered surveillance and security systems. They enable wireless communication between surveillance cameras, sensors, and central control units, facilitating real-time monitoring, data transmission, and intelligent decision-making based on the captured information.

AI Infrastructure: Microstrip patch antennas are also used within the AI infrastructure, such as data centers or server farms. They provide wireless connectivity between AI servers, storage systems, and networking equipment, enabling efficient communication and coordination of resources for AI processing and analysis.

Some of the applications where microstrip patch antennas are employed in the context of artificial intelligence. The wireless connectivity they provide is essential for enabling data exchange, communication, and coordination in AI systems across various domains. Now researchers are trying to explore the new generation emitters and detectors with new materials and new processing devices with new frontiers THz spectrum. Now the research is going on the healthcare development with THz applications.

The paper [32] has reviewed the THz imaging and sensing techniques for different medical applications. It has shown the path of invention and optimization of THz techniques and biosensors. It has explained the THz imaging, production and diagnosis and use of metamaterials in patch antenna. It has also defined THz 4.0 techniques for upcoming advance medical system. It has further detected the advantages and drawbacks of THz techniques with corrective suggested measures for upcoming research.

3 Synthetic Neural Networks

In fact, there has been a lengthy history—dating back thousands of years—of the study of the human brain. However, the development of contemporary electronics has resulted in considerable breakthroughs in the industry. The development for the initial artificial neural network (ANN) model by Warren McCulloch and Walter Pitts in 1943 [33] is a significant turning point in this area. This model portrayed electrical circuits as straightforward neural networks, drawing inspiration from the computing power of the human brain.

Research on artificial neural networks has continued to evolve and has contributed significantly to the field of neuroscience and artificial intelligence. Neural networks are designed to mimic the interconnected structure of neurons in the brain and are used for various applications such as pattern recognition, machine learning, and data analysis.

The development of modern electronics and computing power has enabled researchers to simulate more complex neural networks and explore the workings of the human brain in greater detail. These advancements have opened up new possibilities for understanding brain function, cognitive processes, and developing innovative technologies inspired by the brain's computational power.

By using the most basic learning characteristic, ANN is capable of creating and exploring new knowledge without assistance. The functions of learning, association, classification, generalization, feature selection, and generalizations are similar to those of the human brain. Optimizations can be successfully used [34–36].

A comparative study has done with various literatures in the Table-1 above. They are applied for different applications like skin cancer detection, Health monitoring, navigation, Wimax and WLAN etc. Wireless capsule endoscopy, In this comparison it is shown that [15] produces the maximum bandwidth for wireless capsule endoscopy applications but [17] is more miniaturized in size with comparison to other literature.

There are many literatures which have provide many more information regarding in this field.

Table 1. Comparison between various Literature antennas

Ref.	Center Freq (GHz)	B.W (GHz)	Substrate	Size (mm^2)	Application
[10]	0.275	–	RT/Duroid 5880 (εr = 3.4, t = 0.254 mm)	100 × 75	Skin Cancer detection
[11]	2.45	–	Leather textile (εr = 1.8, t = 2 mm)	38 × 29.4	Health monitoring, navigation, Mobile computing and public safety
[13]	2.3 and 2.66	1	FR-4 (εr = 4.4, t = 1.57 mm) and Denim material (εr = 1.67, t = 0.5	45.25 × 20.60	Remote Health monitoring
[14]	2.45	0.1	FR-4 (εr = 4.4, t = 1.57 mm)	40 × 40	Microwave hyperthermia treatment
[15]	5.45	5.11	FR-4 (εr = 4.3, t = 1.572 mm)	10 × 10	Wireless capsule endoscopy
[16]	0.433	0.175	FR-4 (εr = 4.3, t = 1.6 mm)	8.715 × 7.79	Wireless capsule endoscopy
[17]	0.915	0.3	Silicon ((εr = 11.9, t = 0.675 mm))	7 × 7	Wireless capsule endoscopy
[20]	3.5	0.1	FR-4 (εr = 4.3, t = 1.55 mm)	39.85 × 36.70	Wimax and WLAN

Research paper [37] has designed a 2 × 2 patch antenna array using FR-4, Roger, Air, Glass_pyrex and ceramic substrate materials for Ku band biomedical applications.

The circular polarized simulated antenna has results of 60% Axial Ratio bandwidth and greater than 15dBi gain on these substrate materials using Right-hand Circular polarization (RHCP) technique. Cross-polarization effect has been suppressed using cross-polarized suppressor using cross pol suppressor. The substrate material of low dielectric constant substrate materials have been used for high gain and low VSWR, return loss (Table 1).

Designed patch antenna of research paper [38] has hexagon structure on a polyimide substrate of dielectric constant 3.5 for ultra-wideband 2THz frequency. The feedline has been used microstrip line and a quarter-wave transformer for power source to antenna. To reduce the back radiation and cross-polarization, partial ground plane has been used. The simulated results have 7.96 dBi gain, 0.34 THz to 2.4 THz ultrawideband impedance bandwidth (IMBW) and 98% maximum radiation efficiency for spectroscopic detection and diagnosis, imaging system, sensing, biomedical imaging, and indoor wireless communication system.

Research paper [39, 40] has designed monopole antenna for S and C Frequency band. Dual wideband antenna structure has two symmetrical L-shaped strips, a hexagonal-shaped radiator and a rectangular stub in the CPW ground plane. Simulated Antenna has a range of impedance bandwidth (IBW) from 80% (1.4–3.3 GHz) to 43.90% (4.8–7.5GHz), and ARBW 52.17% (1.7–2.9 GHz) and 25.21% (5.2–6.7 GHz) with a maximum gain of about 3.5 dBi and 5.9 dBi in dual bands, for RHCP radiations.

4   Conclusion

Microstrip antennas have indeed found applications ranging from medical to missile and space applications due to their compact size, cost-effectiveness, and simple fabrication process. In recent research, the performance of various designs has been examined to assess their capabilities. Notably, a resonant frequency of up to 0.85 THz has been achieved using a graphene substrate with a reduced antenna size of 150 μm in length and width. However, it is worth noting that as the frequency requirements increase, the size constraints of microstrip antennas pose challenges and can contribute to increased costs. When designing microstrip antennas for higher resonant frequencies, the size limitation becomes a significant factor in their costliness. Researchers are currently focused on finding ways to maintain cost efficiency while achieving higher resonant frequencies. By exploring innovative materials, design techniques, and fabrication processes, researchers aim to overcome the size constraint challenges and develop cost-effective microstrip antennas capable of operating at higher frequencies. These advancements are crucial for expanding the application potential of microstrip antennas in various industries while keeping them affordable and efficient.

References

1. Auston, D.: Picosecond optoelectronic switching and gating in silicon. Appl. Phys. Lett. **26**(3), 101 (2008)

2. Saeidi, T. Ismail, I. Alhawari, A. R. H. Sali, A. and Ismail, A.: high gain dual-band couple feed transparent THz antenna for satellite communications. In: IEEE Asia-Pacific Conference on Applied Electromagnetics, APACE 2016, Langkawi, Kedah, Malaysia, 11–13 December 2016, pp. 11–15 (2016)
3. Lieber, C.A., Majumder, S.K., Billheimer, D.: Raman micro spectroscopy for skin cancer detection in vitro. J. Biomed. Opt. 13(2), 24013 (2008)
4. Lassau, N. Mercier, S. Koscielny, S.: Prognostic value of high-frequency sonography and color doppler. AJR Am J Roentgenol. 172(2), 457–61 (1999). https://doi.org/10.2214/ajr. 172.2.9930803. PMID: 993080
5. Vilana, et al.: Sonography for the preoperative assessment of melanomas. AJR Am. J. Roentgenol. 172, 457–461 (1999)
6. Abuzaghleh, O., Barkana, B.D., Faezpour, M.: Noninvasive real-time automated skin lesion analysis system for melanoma early detection and prevention. Int. J. Transit. Eng. Health Med. 3, 1–12 (2015)
7. El Fatimi, S.A., Saadi, B.A.: UWB antenna with circular patch for earley breast cancer detection. Telecommun. Comput. Electron. Control 17(5), 2370–2377 (2019)
8. Bhattacharyya, R., Floerkemeier, C., Sarma, S.: Low-cost, ubiquitous RFID-tag-antenna-based sensing. Proc. IEEE 2010(98), 1593–1600 (2010)
9. Tentzeris, M.M., Georgiadis, A., Roselli, L.: Energy harvesting and scavenging. Proc. IEEE 102, 1644–1648 (2014)
10. Occhiuzzi, C., Caizzone, S., Marrocco, G.: Passive UHF RFID antennas for sensing applications: Principles, methods, and classifcations. IEEE Ant. Propagat. Maga. 55(6), 14–34 (2013)
11. Thomas, D.R., Prabhu, V., Sundari, V.K., Kotteshwari, D., Sharanya, K.S.: Design and implementation of z-shaped polarized micro strip patch antenna for detecting skin cancer. In: 2nd International Conference on Smart Technologies and Systems for Next Generation Computing (ICSTSN), Villupuram, India, pp. 1–6 (2023). https://doi.org/10.1109/ICSTSN57873. 2023.10151631, (2023)
12. Bhumireddy, M.E.K., Chanthirasekaran, K.: Implementation of wearable micro-strip patch antenna using leather textile substrate at 2.45 ghz for gain improvement compared to cotton textile substrate antenna. In: AIP Conference Proceedings, vol. 2655, p. 020060 (2023). https://doi.org/10.1063/5.0116522
13. Utkarsh, P., Parulpreet, S., Raghvendra, S.: Review on miniaturized flexible wearable antenna with SAR measurement for body area network. Mater. Today Proc. 66(8), 3667–3674 (2022)
14. Rekha, P., Sumathi, S., Kaushik, S., Kiran, B., Chidananda, S.: Wearable antenna for remote health monitoring. In: International Conference on Intelligent and Innovative Technologies in Computing, Electrical and Electronics (IITCEE) (2023)
15. Komalpreet, K. Amanpreet, K.: Archimedes spiral antenna for the microwave hyperthermia application. In: 3rd International Conference on Smart Electronics and Communication (ICOSEC) (2022)
16. Hammed, M.A.N., Fayadh, R.A., Farhan, H.M.: UWB pentagonal shaped fractal patch antenna for wireless capsule endoscopy. The Fourth Scientific Conference for Engineering and Postgraduate Research, Baghdad, Iraq, 16–17 December 2019 (2019)
17. Biswas, B., Karmakar, A., Chandra, V.: Miniaturized antenna for wireless capsule endoscopy system. In: IEEE MTT-S International Microwave and RF Conference (IMaRC 2019), at IIT Mumbai, 13–15 December 2019 (2019)
18. Biswas, B. Karmakar, A. and Chandra, V. Miniaturised wideband ingestible antenna for wireless capsule endoscopy. IET microwaves, antennas and propagation, 14 (4) pp. 293–301, 25th March (2020), England, (2020)

19. Elangovan, S., Gokul Raj, R., Vethaprasath, M., Mahendran, K.: Design and analyzing of hexagon-shaped microstrip patch antenna for biomedical applications. In: International Conference on Computer Communication and Informatics (ICCCI), Coimbatore, India, pp. 1–5 (2023). https://doi.org/10.1109/ICCCI56745.2023.10128199
20. Samy, M.R.K.M., Gudipalli, A.: A review on miniature bio-implant antenna performance enhancement and impact analysis on body fluids in medical application. Measur. Sensors **28**, 100849 (2023)
21. Sadid, Md. S. Shahriar, S. Mahamat, A.: A Comparative analysis on finding out electrolytes from effective data sets in human sweat (2022). hdl.handle.net/123456789/1623
22. Abozied, A., Abdelaziz, D., Cihat, Ş: Performance analysis rectangular patch antenna 3.5 GHz for Wi-Max and WLAN: micro-strip patch antenna for for Wi-Max and WLAN. J. Millimeterwave Commun. Optim. Modelling **2**(2), 89–93 (2022)
23. Akila, N., Mohan, P., Indhumathi, K.: Millimetre wave antenna for biomedical applications-a review. In: Journal of Physics Conference Series, International Conference on Material Science, Mechanics and Technology (ICMMT 2022), vol. 2484 (2022)
24. Kim, S., et al.: No battery required: perpetual RFID-enabled wireless sensors for cognitive intelligence applications. IEEE Microw. Mag. **2013**(14), 66–77 (2013)
25. Chen, T., Tian, G.Y., Sophian, A., Que, P.W.: Feature extraction and selection for defect classification of pulsed eddy current. NDT. NdtE Int. **2008**(41), 467–476 (2008)
26. Dobmann, G., Altpeter, I., Sklarczyk, C., Pinchuk, R.: Non-destructive testing with micro-and mm-waves—where we are—where we go. Weld. World **2012**(56), 111–120 (2012)
27. Carvalho, N.B., et al.: Wireless power transmission: R&D activities within Europe. IEEE Trans. Microw. Theory Tech. **2014**(62), 1031–1045 (2014)
28. Finkenzeller, K.: RFID Handbook: Fundamentals and Applications in Contactless Smart Card, Radio Frequency Identification and Near-Field Communication, 3rded. Wiley, Wiltshire (2010)
29. Li, S.C., Xu, L.D., Zhao, S.S.: The internet of things: a survey. Inf. Syst. Front. **2015**(17), 243–259 (2015)
30. Al-Fuqaha, A., Guizani, M., Mohammadi, M., Aledhari, M., Ayyash, M.: Internet of things a survey on enabling technologies, protocols, and applications. IEEE Commun. Surv. Tutor. **2015**(17), 2347–2376 (2015)
31. Song, G., Zhang, B., Lyu, Y., Sun, T., Wang, X., He, C.: Application of frequency doubling in micro-strip patch antenna for wireless strain detection. Sens. Actu. A: Phys. **321**, 11403 (2021)
32. Venkataramanan, C., Porchelvi, N.J., Martin, S., Subramanian, P., Jaya, S.: Diamond shaped micro-strip fractal antenna for ultra-wideband. In: International Conference on Edge Computing and Applications (ICECAA) (2022)
33. Mavis, G., Ghanshyam, S.: Terahertz imaging and sensing for healthcare: current status and future perspectives. IEEE Access **11**, 18590–18619 (2023)
34. Warner, B., Misra, M.: Understanding neural networks as statistical tools. Am. Stat. **50**(4), 284-293S (1996)
35. Masters, T.: Practical Neural Network Recipes. Academic Press Inc., London (1993)
36. Deepshikha, S., Bimal Raj, D.: Design of microwave imaging based microstrip ultra-wideband antenna. In: IEEE Conference INDICON (2015)
37. Siraj, Y., Alaoui, K.S., Jaouad, F.: Study and design of a patch antenna for biomedical applications. In: ITM Web of Conferences, vol. 52, p. 03003. COCIA (2023). https://doi.org/10.1051/itmconf/20235203003
38. Kalra, B., Sharma, M.M., Singh, G., Mukherjee, S., Garg, J., Vyas, S.: Material analysis of sequentially rotated 2× 2 patch antenna array. Mater. Today: Proc. **74**, 156–160 (2023). https://doi.org/10.1016/j.matpr.2022.08.038

39. Choudhary, J., Kalra, B., Vyas, S., Nayyar, A., Sharma, M., Ghanshyam, S.: Modified hexagonal shaped ultra-wideband THz antenna. Association for Computing Machinery (2023). https://doi.org/10.1145/3603781.3603840
40. Jaiverdhan, M., Sharma, M., Dhara, R., Sharma, I.B., Kalra, B., Vyas, S.: Design of L-shaped strip loaded dual band hexagonal shaped circularly polarized monopole antenna. In: 2021 IEEE Indian Conference on Antennas and Propagation (InCAP), Jaipur, Rajasthan, India, pp. 929–932 (2021). https://doi.org/10.1109/InCAP52216.2021.9726263

An Optimal Design of an MLFNN Coupled with Genetic Algorithm for Prediction of MIG-CO$_2$ Welding Process

Susmita Roy[1]($\boxtimes$) (iD), Banya Das[1] (iD), Biswajit Das[2] (iD), and Paritosh Bhattacharya[1] (iD)

[1] National Institute of Technology Agartala, Agartala 799046, Tripura, India
susmitaroy.nita@gmail.com
[2] Tripura Institute of Technology, Narsingarh, Tripura, India

Abstract. In this paper, an optimal design of multilayer feed forward neural network coupled with real coded genetic algorithm has been demonstrated for predictive modeling of MIG-CO$_2$ welding process parameters for EN-3A grade mild steel. The predictive modeling of this procedure has been established in the forward direction by designing a multilayer neural network model through updating its connection weights by back propagation algorithm and by real-coded genetic algorithm on the data set which was collected experimentally. Finally, a comparison study on the most efficient neural network design using Python programming has been carried out, and it was discovered that the multiple regression model and the back propagation neural network (BPNN) are both outperformed by the welding geometry predicted by the genetic algorithm tuned neural network (GANN) model.

Keywords: MIG-CO$_2$ welding · Multi Layer Feed Forward Neural Network · Genetic Algorithm

1 Introduction and Literature Review

Welding is the most well-liked joining process in the manufacturing industries because of its extensively used fabrication process, due to its strength equal or greater than that of the foundation metal. The automatic characteristics of any welded joint are significantly influenced by the weld bead geometry. As a result, choosing the right welding settings is essential for producing the ideal weld bead shape [1, 2]. Many mathematical models have been researched in the literature to manage weld productivity, quality, microstructure, and characteristics during the arc welding process [3]. In addition to Taguchi's method, Montgomery [4] added an original orthogonal array design to examine each process parameter with a limited number of experiments. The Response Surface Methodology was utilized by Benjounis et al. [5] to link the laser welding input parameters to the outcomes of an AISI 304 stainless steel butt joint. Murugan et al. [6] developed a 4 factors, 5 levels factorial technique to predict the geometry of the weld-bead prior to the deposition of 316L stainless steel onto structural steel IS 2062. To predict the form of the

R. C. Bansal et al. (Eds.): ACTET 2023, CCIS 2000, pp. 82–95, 2024.
https://doi.org/10.1007/978-3-031-54162-9_6

weld beads, Ganjigatti [7] employed statistical regression analysis. Using a statistical regression model constructed on the basis of a full-factorial design of trials, Casalino [8] investigated MIG- laser CO2 hybrid welding of Al-Mg alloy. Ganjigatti et al. [9, 10] have investigated the MIG welding input–output connections using regression analysis.

In order to address the issue of modeling manufacturing processes with many inputs and outputs, ANNs have received significant attention from researchers in this field in recent years. Andersen et al. [11] created neural network modeling of the arc welding procedure. Cook [12] first focused on developing intelligent welding control systems based on ANNs. Juang et al. [13] examined the back- and counter-propagation networks in attempt to establish a connection between the process parameters and the properties of the bead shape. An ANN model was developed by Ghosal et al. [14] to forecast and enhance the CO2 laser MIG hybrid welding penetration depth for 5005 Al-Mg alloy. The bead form of mild steel electrodes positioned on cast iron plates was estimated using BPNN by Nagesh et al. [15]. Lee et al.'s [16] significant use of BPNNs for parameter prediction in several welding processes.A neural network was used by Kim et al. [17] to model the GMA welding bead form. Inputs into the network are three, and output is one. Regression analysis, BPNN, and genetic neural system (i.e., GANN) all outperformed one another when Dutta et al. [18] compared their efficiency in replicating the TIG welding procedure to the GANN.

In their research, Treutler et al. [20] have provided a general overview and modeling of the wire arc additive manufacturing (WAAM) process for several materials. Ji et al.'s [21] solution to the issue of cracks developing in furnace shells as a result of the furnace's rapid cooling involved combining the grey relational analysis method with back propagation neural networks and genetic algorithms. To address the issue of deterioration of insulation capacity of mineral oil transformers, Soni et al. [22] combined the effects of fuzzy logic controller and fuzzy clustering methods. Madavi et al. [23] investigated how activated flux affected the tensile strength of mild steel during the MIG welding process.

2 Experiments and Data Collection

British Standard 970's grade "EN-3A" black rolled or forged carbon steel is used for the experimentation. British Standard's corresponding code for EN-3A is 070M20. This material was developed primarily for light-duty pulleys, flanges, bushes, spacers, low-tensile shafts, bolts, nuts, and machinery parts where low-tensile strength material is required. Table 1 displays the chemical make-up of the work piece and the electrode material.

Table 1. Chemical composition of the base metal and the electrode, wt%

	C	Mn	S	P	Si
Base Metal	0.15	0.78	0.021	0.029	0.23
Electrode	0.16	0.76	0.020	0.026	0.22

The work piece for each experiment was a pair of EN-3A steel specimens that were 150 mm × 100 mm × 6 mm in size. The root face, root gap, and groove angle of these specimens—which had a V-shaped groove drilled into them—were measured, respectively, at 3 mm, 0.75 mm, and 30°. Then, 24 pairs of these specimens were created with a consistent groove angle, a root face, and faces that had been surface-ground clean. To produce a butt joint, two plates were joined at the ends along the width while maintaining the root gap at 0.75 mm. After the welding was finished, a power hacksaw was used to cut each plate to the precise shape needed for depth of penetration measurement. The portable gas cutting machine, which has a fixed arm and can move at various known speeds, had a welding torch installed on it. The electrode in the experiment was a 1.2 mm diameter wire coated in copper made of mild steel. A roller drive system supplied the wire through the welding gun. CO_2 was used as the shielding gas, which was delivered in a controlled manner at a constant flow rate and pressure. The partial-factorial design of experiments has been used to gather the input-output data. With three input process parameters with five levels for each, there are $5^3 = 125$ possible combinations of the input parameters. However, in the current study, five levels of parameters are used, and 25 combinations of input process parameters are used to conduct the tests. Table 2 displays five parameter levels.

Table 2. Selected levels for welding parameters

Parameter	Unit	Level				
		1	2	3	4	5
Current(I)	Ampere	140	150	160	170	180
Voltage(V)	Volt	24	25	26	27	28
Weldingspeed(S)	m/min	0.165	0.179	0.193	0.206	0.220

3 Techniques for Analysis

Non-linear statistical regression analysis and neural networks have been used in input-output modeling, as detailed below:

3.1 Regression Analysis

In order to forecast the DP, MDR, and WH using the experimental data, the data gathered from the experimental runs has undergone a non-linear regression analysis. The following equation illustrates how the response and input process parameters have a nonlinear relationship.

$$Z = \gamma_0 + \sum_{i=1}^{k} \gamma_i Z_i + \sum_{i=1}^{k} \gamma_{ii} Z_i^2 + \sum_{i=1}^{k} \sum_{i<j}^{k} \gamma_{ii} Z_i Z_j + \varepsilon \qquad (1)$$

where ε stands for the fitting error. The equation above includes linear components like $Z_1, Z_2, \ldots, Z_k$; squared terms such as $Z_1^2, Z_2^2, \ldots, Z_k^2$; and the interaction terms such as $Z_1 Z_2, Z_2 Z_3, \ldots, Z_{k-1} Z_k$. The coefficients, i.e., γ values, can be calculated using the least-squares error concept.

3.2 Neural Networks-Based Methods

The process of forward mapping is carried out using neural network-based methods, as discussed below:

For the current issue, neural network-based methods are utilized to create models that predict the depth of penetration (D), rate of material deposition (R), and width of the HAZ zone (WHZ) for the MIG-CO_2 welding process parameters with mild steel of EN-3A grade. As detailed below, two neural network-based strategies have been created.

Back Propagation Neural Network (BPNN) Modeling

In this study, a three-layered BPNN has been constructed to forecast the process variables and performance of the MIG-CO_2 welding process. This is because three-layered neural networks with back propagation weight updates are capable of accurately mapping any non-linear relationship. In order to analyze the forward model, the three input neurons and three output neurons are considered. The linking weights, which have values ranging from 0.0 to 1.0 and are determined at random, are indicated by the symbols [V] and [W] for the linking weights between the input and hidden layers and [V] and [W] for the linking weights between the output and hidden layers, respectively. For the input, hidden, and output layers, the transfer functions are assumed to be linear, tan-sigmoid, and log-sigmoid, respectively. Figure 1 demonstrates a neural network used in forward modelling in schematic form.

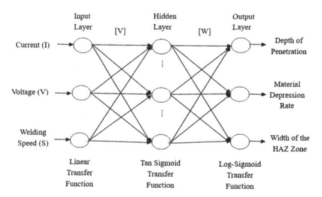

Fig. 1. Diagrammatic View of an MLFFNN

The prediction error at output layer of the kth neuron for a certain training scenario (say l^{th}) is expressed as follows:

$$E_k = \frac{1}{2}(T_k - O_k)^2 \tag{2}$$

where T_k and O_k stand for the intended and expected values of the output, respectively. As V and W are the functions of E, the error E associated with a specific training scenario can be visualized as follows:

$$E_k = f(V, W)$$

The steepest descent approach was used in a BP algorithm to minimize the error E_k, and the alterations to the connecting weight values were determined as follows:

$$\Delta V = -\eta \frac{\partial E_k}{\partial V} \tag{3}$$

$$\Delta W = -\eta \frac{\partial E_k}{\partial W} \tag{4}$$

Now $\frac{\partial E_k}{\partial V}$ and $\frac{\partial E_k}{\partial W}$ could be obtained using the chain rule for differentiation, η denotes the range of learning rates between 0.0 and 1.0. It is referred to as the delta rule. It is vital to note that the slower rate of convergence, which results in a smoother network, the smaller the value of η, the smoother the network will be. On the other hand, while a higher value of η will hasten convergence, the resulting network may start to sag.

Network Performance Criterion
In terms of mean square error (MSE), the MLFNN's performance after being trained using the BP algorithm is defined by Eq. (5).

$$MSE = \frac{1}{L} \frac{1}{P} \sum\nolimits_{l=1}^{L} \sum\nolimits_{k=1}^{P} \frac{1}{2}(T_{kl} - O_{kl})^2 \tag{5}$$

where P stands for the quantity of output neurons, L for the quantity of training scenarios, and T_{kl} and O_{kl} for the goal and predicted output values, respectively.

Genetic Algorithm Neural Network (GANN) Modeling
Based on the natural genetics premise, GA is a stochastic global search and computational optimization scheme [19]. It is useful for a range of tasks in the field of neural networks, including constructing a network's structure and training linking weights. The schematic diagram of the GANN system employed in this investigation is shown in Fig. 2.

A result, real-coded genetic algorithm (GA) has been utilized in this study instead of the back propagation (BP) technique of the BPNN to train neural network and update the linking weights. Using a random number generator, the initial set of solutions (or initial population of the GA) was generated. For each solution, the fitness value is calculated. The reproduction operator known as roulette wheel selection (Brindle, 1981) has been used. Simulated binary crossover (SBX) (Deb, 1995) has been utilizedto generate children solutions. A modified solution was created from an initial solution using polynomial mutation (Deb and Goyal, 1996). Here is a detailed explanation of these operators:

Roulette Wheel Selection
Roulette selection is a stochastic selection technique in which the likelihood of choosing a person depends on how suitable they are. The approach borrows from actual roulettes

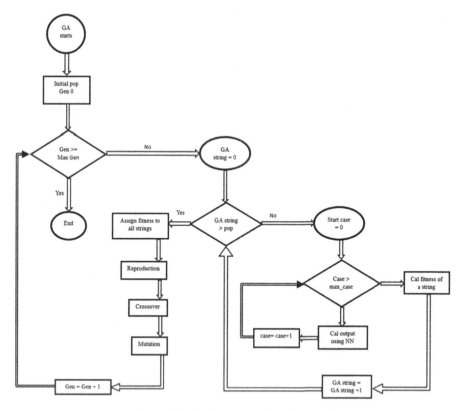

Fig. 2. Flowchart representation of GANN

but also has significant differences from them. In response to the fitness values $f_1, f_2,$ $..., f_N$, the population size N is used to divide the top surface area of the wheel into N sections. Once the wheel has stopped spinning in one direction, the winning area is indicated by a fixed pointer.

According to probability, a specific sub-area that represents a GA-solution is selected as the winner, and the probability that the ith area will be declared the winner is given by the following expression:

$$p = \frac{f_i}{\sum_{i=1}^{N} f_i} \tag{6}$$

The pointer selects the winning region after N rotations or spins of the wheel, with each time only one area being chosen.

Simulated Binary Crossover
If Par_1 and Par_2 are the two parent solutions corresponding to a variable, the children solutions are calculated by the following formula:

$$Ch_1 = 0.5[(Par_1 + Par_2) - \alpha'|Par_2 - Par_1|] \tag{7}$$

$$Ch_2 = 0.5[(Par_1 + Par_2) + \alpha'|Par_2 - Par_1|] \tag{8}$$

where

$$\alpha' = \begin{cases} (2r)^{1/(q+1)} & \text{if } r \leq 0.5 \\ (\frac{1}{2(1-r)})^{\frac{1}{(q+1)}} & \text{if } r > 0.5 \end{cases} \tag{9}$$

Here, q is non-negative real number and r represents a random number lying between 0 and 1.

Polynomial Mutation
From the original solution, the modified solution has been identified as follows:

$$Par_{mutated} = Par_{original} + (\delta \times \delta_{max}) \tag{10}$$

where

$$\delta = \begin{cases} (2r)^{1/(q+1)} - 1 & \text{if } r \leq 0.5 \\ 1 - (2(1-r))^{\frac{1}{(q+1)}} & \text{if } r > 0.5 \end{cases} \tag{11}$$

The maximum user-defined perturbation permitted between the original and modified solutions in this scenario is indicated by δ_{max} and is an exponent (non-negative real number) called q.

The NN represented by a GA-string has been trained in batch mode. The fitness f for a GA-string is calculated using the MSE in predicting the answers and is expressed as follows:

$$f = \frac{1}{L} \frac{1}{P} \sum_{l=1}^{L} \sum_{k=1}^{P} \frac{1}{2}(T_{kl} - O_{kl})^2 \tag{12}$$

When an artificial neural network is developed utilizing GA, the fitness of the ith particle, which is made up of the network's weights as variables, is expressed in terms of its capacity to lower the MSE and is represented by Eq. (13)

$$f_i = \frac{1}{1 + MSE} \tag{13}$$

All strings found in the GA-population have their fitness values calculated. The GA-string population (i.e., NN) is then altered by applying the operators of reproduction, crossover, and mutation. Through search, the GA will attempt to establish an ideal NN.

4   Results and Discussion

The results of input-output mappings for MIG-C02 welding of mild steel of EN-3A grade using regression analysis and neural network-based techniques are discussed in this part. A parametric study is conducted to identify the number of hidden neurons in the network, learning rate, coefficients of transfer for weight updating of the hidden and output layers, maximum number of iterations, and bias value in order to make the best prediction of the MIG-C02 welding process made of EN-3A grade mild steel. Python programming is used to train the specified ANN architecture.

4.1 The Regression Modeling

During regression analysis, a significance test was run on each response to make sure the model was accurate. The process parameters, DP, MDR, and WHZ, which represent the bead geometric parameters, are established as independent parameters, and the equations in Eqs. (14)–(16) using MINITAB 17 statistical software, show the link between the welding parameters.

Depth of Penetration (DP) $= 68.3 - 0.437 \times Y_1 - 4.56 \times Y_2$

$+302 \times Y_3 + 0.00075 \times Y_1^2 + 0.085 \times Y_2^2 + 587 \times Y_3^2 + 0.0181 \times Y_1 \times Y_2$ (14)

$-1.28 \times Y_1 \times Y_3 - 13.4 \times Y_2 \times Y_3$

Material Deposition Rate (MDR) $= 413 - 2.97 \times Y_1 - 29.5 Y_2$

$+2186 Y_3 + 0.00529 \times Y_1^2 + 0.525 \times Y_2^2 + 2940 \times Y_3^2 + 0.1066 \times Y_1 \times Y_2$ (15)

$-7.85 \times Y_1 \times Y_3 - 79 \times Y_2 \times Y_3$

Width of HAZ zone (WHZ) $= 22.4 - 0.1279 \times Y_1 - 1.41 \times Y_2 + 97.1 \times Y_3$

$+0.000296 \times Y_1^2 + 0.0292 \times Y_2^2 + 305.9 \times Y_3^2 + 0.00721 \times Y_1 \times Y_2$

$-0.626 \times Y_1 \times Y_3 - 5.53 \times Y_2 \times Y_3$

$$(16)$$

where Y_1 represents welding current (I), Y_2 represents voltage (V) and Y_3 represents welding speed (S). ANOVA is used to demonstrate the mathematical model's suitability. The findings show that weld parameters were the key factor in responses for things like butt-welded joint penetration depth, material deposition rate, and HAZ breadth. The outcomes of two neural network-based forward mapping methods are listed and described below:

Normalization of the Dataset

Regression analysis has been used to construct one twenty-five (125) sets of data for this investigation. Of those, 120 sets have been used for ANN testing, while the remaining sets have been considered for ANN training. Using the following Eq. (17), normalization is carried out for each parameter in the range of 0.1 to 0.9.

$$y = 0.1 + 0.8 * \left(\frac{x - x_{min}}{x_{max} - x_{min}} \right), \tag{17}$$

where, x = real value

y = the x-value normalised.

x_{max} = maximum parameter value in the dataset.

x_{min} = minimum parameter value in the dataset.

Results of BPNN Modeling

A systematic parametric analysis was carried out in order to thoroughly evaluate the impact of individual parameters on the optimization efficiency of our suggested neural network models. The learning rate, the number of hidden neurons in the network, the coefficient of transfer function for both the hidden and output layers, and the bias of the neural network were the four main factors that were the focus of this study. We attempted to clarify each component's influence on the optimization process and finally direct the choice of optimal configurations by independently changing each parameter while holding the others constant. The learning rate, the number of hidden neurons, the coefficient of transfer function, and the bias value were all set at values that fell between the ranges of 4 to 19, 0.1 to 1, 0.5 to 4.5, and 0.00001 to 0.00010, respectively. In this instance, only one parameter is altered while leaving the rest unchanged. This ensured that the parameter ranges were uniformly chosen for the purpose of controlled study. The observations of BPNN study are shown in Fig. 3(a)–(f).

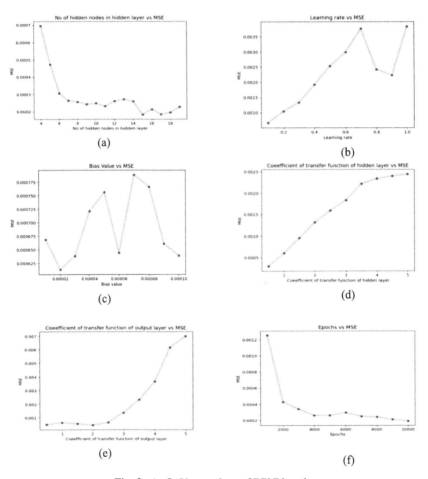

Fig. 3. (a–f) Observations of BPNN study

The neural network topology with fifteen hidden neurons clearly exhibits the lowest Mean Squared Error (MSE) of 0.0002 during the training phase, according to the data from Fig. 3(a–f). As a result, we decide that the architecture designated as 3-15-3 is the best layout for the BPNN model created to handle the unique difficulties of our research. The chosen configuration is then used for all ensuing testing activities. Our analysis also shows that the ideal hyper parameters consist of a learning rate of 0.1, a coefficient of the transfer function in the hidden layer (a_1) of 0.5, a coefficient of the transfer function in the output layer (a_2) of 1, an epoch count of 10,000, and a bias value of 0.00002. These hyper parameters work together to improve the BPNN model's performance and resilience in tackling the complexity of the current inquiry.

GANN Modeling Outcomes

In this section, the optimum network is thoroughly investigated and the parametric investigation for the GANN is presented in Fig. 4(a–c). The parameters of population size (N), maximum number of generations, and hidden neuron number all are adapted in the ranges of (4, 19), (200–290), and (500–5000), respectively.

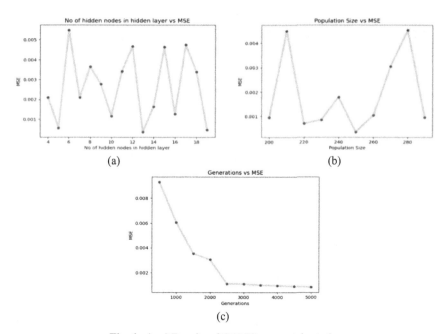

Fig. 4. (**a-c**) Results of GANN-parametric study

The optimal network architecture is achieved with 13 hidden neurons using GANN. With population size of 250 and maximum generations of 5000, the best fitness value is attained. Test cases were run through the GANN that has been optimized, and mean squared errors in output parameter predictions were collected.

Convergence Comparison Between BPNN and GANN Architecture During Training and Testing

Performance of GANN is compared with BPNN model using training and testing MSE in this section. Table 3 displays the results in tabulated form.

Table 3. Comparison between BPNN and GANN

Sl. No.	NN Model	NN Architecture	MSE (Training)	MSE (Testing)	Iteration Number
1	BPNN	3-15-3	0.000682	0.000337	10,000
2	GANN	3-13-3	0.000473	0.000349	5000

Table 3 shows that BPNN gives predicted result with fifteen hidden neurons having training MSE as 0.000682 and testing MSE as 0.000337 for the present problem. And GA trained NN gives predicted result with thirteen hidden neurons having training MSE as 0.000473 and testing MSE as 0.000349 i.e., the GA trained NN gives enhanced prediction results (testing MSE) in a smaller number of iterations compared to BPNN. Figure 5(a) and 5(b) shows graph of number of iterations versus training MSE and testing MSE respectively for the two NN models.

Figure 5(b) shows graph of number of iterations versus testing MSE for the two NN models. It is evident that in testing MSE, GANN model performs better than BPNN as the fluctuation rate of MSE in BPNN, at each iteration, is higher in comparison to GANN.

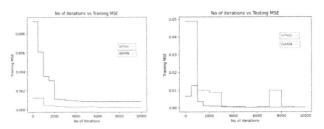

Fig. 5. (a) Comparison of training MSE for BPNN and GANN models (b) Comparison of testing MSE for BPNN and GANN models

Comparison of GANN with BPNN and Regression Models

With the help of the following Eq. (18), an absolute percentage error is calculated to compare performance of the ANN and regression models.

Absolute percentage error in prediction

$$= \left| \frac{\text{Experimental result} - \text{Predicted values of ANN (or, Regression model)}}{\text{Experimental result}} \right| \times 100$$

(18)

Table 4 shows the comparison between regression models and ANN models predicted values of the response parameters with test data.

Table 4. Comparison of regression models with the ANN models

Exp. No.	Experimental Output			Predicted output with regression testing			Predicted output with BPNN model (De normalized value)			Predicted output with GANN testing (De normalized value)		
	DP (mm)	MDR (g/min)	WH (mm)	DP (mm)	MDR (g/min)	WH (mm)	DP (mm)	MDR (g/min)	WH (mm)	DP (mm)	MDR (g/min)	WH (mm)
1	5.1	1.7134	5.3285	5.063	1.856	5.274	5.152	1.740	5.362	5.067	1.768	5.329
2	6.9	3.1043	7.3992	7.035	3.224	7.359	6.921	3.103	7.293	6.943	3.049	7.278
3	6.8	2.9021	7.1032	6.809	2.920	7.066	6.780	2.895	7.110	6.789	2.825	7.072
4	6.5	2.4519	6.8497	6.607	2.634	6.796	6.594	2.610	6.893	6.604	2.552	6.864
5	6.4	2.4312	6.6298	6.492	2.483	6.594	6.439	2.369	6.743	6.462	2.351	6.743

Table 5 shows that the mean absolute percentage error for the regression model utilizing Eq. (18) for the responses DP, MDR and WH are 1.179%, 4.480% and 0.683% respectively. And the mean absolute percentage errors for the 3-15-3 BPNN model are calculated as 0.737%, 2.180% and 0.891% respectively, while for 3-13-3 GANN model the mean absolute % errors are 0.803%, 2.985% and 0.803% respectively.

Table 5. Comparison of absolute percentage error of the testing data

Exp. No.	Absolute % error								
	Experimental output with regression output			Experimental output with BPNN model			Experimental output with GANN model		
	DP (mm)	MDR (g/min)	WH (mm)	DP (mm)	MDR (g/min)	WH (mm)	DP (mm)	MDR (g/min)	WH (mm)
1	0.725	8.323	1.023	1.013	1.573	0.622	0.646	3.187	0.014
2	1.957	3.856	0.543	0.305	0.056	1.439	0.629	1.755	1.632
3	0.132	0.627	0.524	0.297	0.260	0.053	0.155	2.630	0.428
4	1.646	7.427	0.784	1.449	6.440	0.638	1.609	4.085	0.219
5	1.437	2.169	0.54	0.620	2.572	1.706	0.975	3.269	1.721
Mean absolute % error	1.179	4.480	0.683	0.737	2.180	0.891	0.803	2.985	0.803

5 Conclusion

This current demonstration aims to estimate the output of MIG-CO_2 welding process parameters with EN-3A grade mild steel by designing a multilayer neural network model in the forward direction. An effort is given to forecast the optimal welding geometry in MIG-CO_2 welded butt joints. According to Taguchi's L_{25} partial-factorial design, all the experiments have been carried out. Two different approaches e.g., BPNN and GANN have been implemented to revise the concerning weights of the said network to get optimal network architecture by developing a python programming. During training of the model, out of several ANN architectures used, 3-13-3 is found to be the most efficient using GANN model (as GA trained NN gives predicted result with thirteen hidden neurons having training MSE as 0.000473 and testing MSE as 0.000349) compared to BPNN model (BPNN gives predicted result with fifteen hidden neurons having training MSE as 0.000682 and testing MSE as 0.000337) in a very a smaller number of iterations. Also, the GANN model is found to predict the output much better (the mean absolute % errors are 0.803%, 2.985% and 0.803% respectively for the three outputs) compared to regression model (the mean absolute % errors are 1.179%, 4.480% and 0.683% respectively) for output.

References

1. Zhang, Y.M., Kovacevic, R., Li, L.: Characterization and real time measurement of geometrical appearance of the weld pool. Int. J. Mach. Tools Manuf. **36**(7), 799–816 (1996)
2. Tarng, Y.S., Yang, W.H.: Optimization of the weld bead geometry in gas Tungsten arc welding by the Taguchi Method. J. Adv. Manuf. Technol. **14**, 549–54 (1998)
3. Feder, D.K.: Computers in welding technology—a look at applications, potentials, welding quality, the role of computers, Vienna, Austria, Pergamon Press, IIW, pp. 17–35 (1988)

4. Montgomery, D.C.: Design and Analysis of Experiments, 2nd edn. Wiley, New York (1984)
5. Benjounis, K.Y., Olabi, A.G., Hasmi, M.S.J.: Multi-response optimization of CO_2 laser welding process of austenitic stainless steel. Opt. Laser Technol. **40**, 76–87 (2008)
6. Murugan, N., Parmar, R.S.: Effects of MIG process parameters on the geometry of the bead in the automatic surfacing of stainless steel. J. Mater. Process. Technol. **41**(4), 381–398 (1994)
7. Ganjigatti, J.P.: Application of statistical methods and fuzzy logic techniques to predict bead geometry in welding, Ph.D. thesis, IIT Kharagpur, India (2006)
8. Casalino, G.: Statistical analysis of MIG-laser CO2 hybrid welding of Al-Mg alloy. J. Mater. Process. Technol. **191**(1), 106–110 (2007)
9. Ganjigatti, J.P., Pratihar, D.K., Choudhury, R.A.: Modeling of the MIG welding process using statistical approaches. Int. J. Adv. Manuf. Technol. **35**, 1166–1190 (2008)
10. Ganjigatti, J.P., Pratihar, D.K., Choudhury, R.A.: Global versus cluster-wise regression analyses for prediction of bead geometry in MIG welding process. J. Mater. Process. Technol. **189**, 352–366 (2007)
11. Andersen, K., Cook, G.E., Karsai, G., Ramaswamy, K.: Artificial neural networks applied to arc welding process modelling and control. IEEE Trans. Ind. Appl. **26**, 824–830 (1990)
12. Cook, G.E.: Feedback and adaptive control in automated arc welding system. Metal Constr. **13**(9), 551–556 (1990)
13. Juang, S.C., Tarng, Y.S., Lii, H.R.: A comparison between the back propagation and counter-propagation networks in the modelling of the TIG welding process. J. Mater. Process Technol. **75**, 54–62 (1998)
14. Ghosal, S., Chaki, S.: Estimation and optimization of depth of penetration in hybrid CO_2 laser-MIG welding using ANN-optimization hybrid model. Int. J. Adv. Manuf. Technol. **47**, 1149–1157 (2010)
15. Nagesh, D.S., Datta, G.L.: Prediction of weld bead geometry and penetration in shielded metal arc welding using artificial neural networks. J. Mater. Process. Technol. **123**, 303–312 (2002)
16. Lee, J.I., Um, K.W.: A prediction of welding process parameters by prediction of back-bead geometry. J. Mater. Process. Technol. **108**(1), 106–113 (2000)
17. Kim, D., Kang, M., Rhee, S.: Determination of optimal welding conditions with a controlled random search procedure. Weld. J. **90**(8), 125–130 (2005)
18. Dutta, P., Pratihar, D.K.: Modeling of TIG welding process using conventional regression analysis and neural network-based approaches. J. Mater. Process. Technol. **184**, 56–68 (2007)
19. Goldberg, D.E.: Genetic Algorithm in Search, Optimization and Machine Learning, pp. 1–21. Pearson Education, Singapore (2001)
20. Treutler, K., Wesling, V.: The current state of Research of Wire Arc Additive Manufacturing (WAAM): a review. Inst. Weld. Mach. Appl. Sci. **11**(18), 8619 (2021)
21. Ji, H., Yuan, J., Huang, X., Yang, X., Liu, S., Wang, B.: Welding process optimization for blast furnace shell by numerical simulation and experimental study. J. Market. Res. **26**, 603–620 (2023)
22. Soni, R., Mehta, B.: Diagnosis and prognosis of incipient faults and insulation status for asset management of power transformer using fuzzy logic controller & fuzzy clustering means. Electr. Power Syst. Res. **220**, 109256 (2023)
23. Madavi, K.R., Jogi, B.F., Lohar, G.S.: Metal inert gas (MIG) welding process: a study of effect of welding parameters. Mater. Today Proc. **51**(1), 690–698 (2022)

Stochastic Model for Estimation of Aggregated EV Charging Load Demand

Akanksha Shukla[1]([✉]) [iD], Abhilash Kumar Gupta[2] [iD], and Kataria Pratik Hemantbhai[1]

[1] Department of Electrical Engineering, SVNIT, Surat, Gujarat 395007, India
ashukla@eed.svnit.ac.in
[2] Counterpoint Technology Market Research, Mumbai, India

Abstract. The transformation of smart cities can be greatly aided by the electrification of transportation. Adoption of Electric Vehicles (EVs) is enhanced by deploying fast charging stations and by providing drivers with the convenience of fast charging their vehicles to full capacity. Prior to installing the charging infrastructure, it is important to assess the EV charging demand. The demand for EV charging at a given station depends on specific characteristics of EVs, the driving patterns, charging rate, location of charging. In this work, a scenario-based temporal stochastic fast EV charging demand is developed considering the uncertainties associated with the aforementioned factors. Model is able to estimate both weekdays and weekends demand where the peak and valleys occur at different time of the day. Monte-Carlo simulation is utilized to model the scenario-based demand. The uncertainties are incorporated into the charging demand estimation by establishing suitable probability density functions (PDF) as per the surveys available from the realistic data. By employing this simulation approach, the model aims to simulate and predict EV owners' charging patterns, enabling a comprehensive evaluation of the expected charging demand at fast charging stations. The model gives interval estimation of the EV charging demand with confidence interval varying from 85% to 99%.

Keywords: Electric vehicles (EVs) · Fast charging stations · Monte Carlo simulation · Probability density functions · Poisson distribution

1 Introduction

With increase greenhouse gas emissions, decline in fossil fuel supplies, and increase in fuel prices, governments around the world have started promoting widespread deployment of Electric Vehicles (EVs) as a viable replacement to gasoline-powered cars. This require upgradation of existing electrical and charging infrastructure [1]. To anticipate the changes required in electrical and transportation infrastructure, it is important to anticipate the charging load demand imposed by the EVs on the grid.

Although acceptance of EV lead to lower carbon emissions, but this will introduce new type load into the grid. The two main classifications of EVs are 1) battery-powered EVs and 2) hybrid EVs (HEVs). More attention is paid to HEVs than other EV types as

© The Author(s), under exclusive license to Springer Nature Switzerland AG 2024
R. C. Bansal et al. (Eds.): ACTET 2023, CCIS 2000, pp. 96–106, 2024.
https://doi.org/10.1007/978-3-031-54162-9_7

they can operate in internal combustion engine and electric mode. One type of HEVs use an internal combustion engine to recharge their batteries, however plug-in HEVs (PHEVs) may recharge their batteries using electrical connections [2]. A suitable charging infrastructure must be established in order to meet the increasing demand for electrical energy made by these cars. Three standard EV charging levels have been suggested by the American Society of Automotive Engineers [3] as listed in Table 1. The AC level 1 and 2 are the home charging stations or the workplace while AC level 3 and DC level require separate charging utility generally known as fast or ultrafast charging stations. Most of the time EVs owners will prefer to charge the EV at home or workplace requiring low to medium charging power requirement and called as uncoordinated charging [4, 5].

Table 1. SAE J1772 Standards for Charging Infrastructure [3]

Charge method	Voltage, AC (V)	Phase	Max. Current	Max. Power
AC Level 1	120	1-phase	15 or 20	1.44 or 1.92
AC Level 2	208 or 240	1-phase	30–100	5.0–19.2
AC Level 3	208–600	3-phase	80–200	22.7–166
DC Level 1	50–1000	--	80	80
DC Level 2	50–1000	--	400	400

The charging demand of EV depends on different uncertain factors such as daily energy requirement which in turn depends on daily driving distance, battery initial State of Charge (SOC), time of the day, location of charging, charging rate [4]. Further, the charging demand modelling can be deterministic [6] or stochastic [7] in nature. Deterministic modelling has lower computation complexity but does not represent uncertainty associated with the different factors. A lot of research has been carried out in this field. Agent-based modelling [8], AI-based modelling [9], incorporation of probabilistic and statistical technique to model the uncertain parameters [5], Markov Chain models [10] and Monte Carlo simulation [11]. Most of the studies have preferred to develop the data-driven models utilizing the transportation data, demography and vehicle type. Uncertain factors such arrival time. Departure time and daily driving distance is modelled using probability distribution functions of which Poisson distribution is the most suitable choice [4]. Further, Cupola method to represent the joint probability of the random variables is also developed [12]. A real data from the recorded charging measurements and the survey were used for analyzing the impact in Korean grid. Questionnaire demonstrated that the EV owners preferred to go for uncoordinated charging at fast charging stations during the peak hours and to meet the range anxiety while going for long-distance trips [13].

Previous studies have used distinct models, factors influencing charging demand and the complexity levels. These diversified model brings difficulty in standardizing the estimation model. These studies are based on the several assumptions without being supported strongly by the mathematical models representing uncertainties. Also, it is observed that demand estimation model is for slow charging EVs is established for carrying out planning of charging stations, impact on the grid and future acceptability of EVs. Thus, it is crucial to develop a comprehensive stochastic estimation model for EV fast charging demand considering different uncertainties. Therefore, this work aims to develop stochastic EV fast charging demand model to assist the policy makers and researchers in making the decision and carrying out various power grid studies. A stochastic EV charging model is developed with uncertainties modelled by introducing random variables using PDFs supported by realistic transportation survey data. The data is derived from transportation survey data, manufacturers data, SAE J1772 standards. Monte Carlo simulations are used to develop scenario-based stochastic model as it an appropriate method to generate the scenarios as reported in the literature. The objectives carried out in this work are:

1. Development of probability distribution of daily driven mileage and probability distribution for both weekdays and weekends, arrival time.
2. Sampling of the above-mentioned probability distribution function for scenario generation and extraction of initial SOC and charging time.
3. Develop expected charging load demand using Monte Carlo simulation.

Paper is organized as: Sect. 2 describes EV charging load profile modelling with inherent uncertainties followed by methodology in Sect. 3. Results and discussions are presented in Sect. 4 and Sect. 5 concludes the paper.

2 Estimation of EV Fast Charging Load Profile

In this section, the stochastic EV fast charging load profile is developed. Charging load profile is modelled for a fast charging station taking into account 500 EVs coming to the charging station and leave it completely charged. Table 2 shows five distinct classes of 500 EVs taken into consideration with their respective battery capacity and share of the fleet. The classification of vehicles and associated AER, as well as the classification of various EV classes, are based on information from the National Household Travel Survey [14]. Here, AER is referred to as a vehicle's electrically powered driving range. Here, electric range of 40, 20, and 10 miles is considered based on projections from the Plug-in hybrid electric car model. It should be emphasized that there is no direct correlation between battery capacity and vehicle size. For instance, an economy car Chevy Volt has more battery capacity of 17.1 kWh compared to 12 kWh for large SUV Mitsubishi Outlander EV.

In this work, charging station demand profile is modelled for a predetermined period by summing demand of individual EVs with the consideration of various uncertain factors. These factors are: distribution of the fleet's various vehicle types, the likelihood of daily driving distance, and the likelihood of driving at any given instant.

Table 2. Parameters of different types of EVs

EVs type-all electric range [mile]	Battery capacity [kWh]	Charging level [kW]	fleet (%)
Car 40	11.2	33.6	29.2
Car 20	5.6	16.8	29.5
Van SUV, light truck 20	6.94	20.82	20.6
Van SUV, light truck 10	3.47	10.41	20.6
Other truck 10	4.34	13.02	0.1

2.1 Estimation of Daily Driven Mileage

For estimating the daily driven mileage, National household travel survey data is utilized which provides the survey of 1,048,576 households and 309,164 vehicles and the driving patterns of the vehicles are obtained from this. Figure 1 shows the weighted probability of daily driven miles. This weighted probability of daily driven miles is used to model the random daily energy requirement variable of each vehicle. Different probability distribution curves are fitted on this daily driven mileage curve and based on the maximum likelihood estimation, best PDF is determined. It is found that lognormal distribution is the best fitted curve. A lognormal distribution is a PDF with a logarithmic normal distribution.

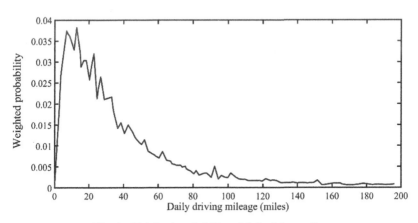

Fig. 1. Weighted probability of daily driven miles

The lognormal distribution is represented by the Eq. (1), μ is the location parameter and σ is the scale parameter. Mean and variance is represented by Eq. (2) and (3) respectively.

$$y = f(x|\mu, \sigma) = \frac{1}{x\sigma\sqrt{2\pi}} e^{\frac{(-logx-\mu)^2}{2\sigma^2}} \quad for \ x > 0 \tag{1}$$

$$m = e^{\left(\mu + \frac{1}{2}\sigma^2\right)} \tag{2}$$

$$v = e^{(2\mu + \sigma^2)(e^{\sigma^2} - 1)} \tag{3}$$

The goodness of fit test is determined and it indicates whether or not the data in the sample matches the data in the actual data. The goodness of fit indices considered in this work are sum of square errors (SSE), root mean square error and R^2. The obtained value of mean and variance of lognormal distribution is found to be mean m = 3.358 and standard deviation = 0.9378 while the goodness of fit indicators are SSE = 1.082 × $10^{-.5}$, RMSE = 0.0003548 and R^2 = 0.9976. The values of SSE and RMSE closer to 0 indicate less error between actual data and the fitted data while R^2 = 1 indicates better fit following the shape. Figure 2 shows the fitted lognormal PDF of weighted probability of daily driven distance.

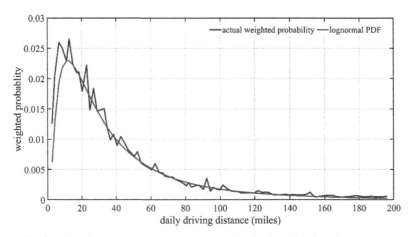

Fig. 2. Fitted lognormal PDF on probability distribution of daily driven mileage

From this lognormal PDF, cumulative distribution function (CDF) is derived given by Eq. (4):

$$CDF = \frac{1}{2}\left[1 + erf\left(\frac{\ln(x - \mu)}{\sigma}\right)\right] \tag{4}$$

where erf is the Gaussian error function. Figure 3 shows the derived daily driving mileage CDF.

The derived CDF is further utilized for sampling the daily driven distance for each EV and scenarios. The continuous CDF is converted into discrete CDF for simplifying the sampling process. Each point in the curve is assumed to be situated inside an interval $[d_i, d_{i+1}]$. Then the sampling is done as per the Roulette wheel selection method where the average mileage d_α is given by Eq. (5) while probability of selecting this average daily mileage from CDF is given by Eq. (6).

$$d_a = \frac{d_i + d_{i+1}}{2} \tag{5}$$

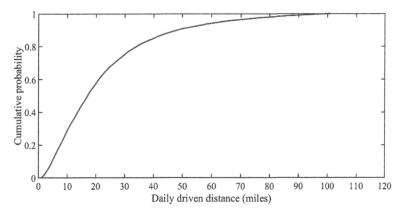

Fig. 3. Cumulative probability of daily driven distance

$$F(d_a) = \int\limits_{d_i}^{d_{i+1}} f(x|\mu, \sigma)dx \tag{6}$$

2.2 Estimation of Temporal Vehicle Distribution

Aggregated EV charging demand model for fast charging EVs with different electric range is developed considering the probability of EV distribution on the road at each time instant. NHTS 2009 data is again used to establish the probability of vehicle distribution on the road during weekdays and weekends to account for both holidays and working days. The probability distribution of vehicle distribution is shown in Fig. 4. According to Fig. 4, there is a 0.01 percent chance that a car will be on the road at 4 o'clock, which is indicated by the likelihood of automobiles at 4th hour g(4) being 1%. From the probability distribution of daily driven trips for weekdays and weekends, CDF is established shown in Fig. 5 and then discretized for sampling the percent of vehicles on the road. This distribution is utilized to sample the number of EVs charging simultaneously.

2.3 Estimation of Charging Demand

To estimate the fast charging demand of EVs, different random variables like daily energy requirement, initial SOC, vehicle types, total vehicles charging simultaneously are modelled using the established PDF from the NHTS data. The CDF of daily driven distance is used to determine the initial SOC and the daily energy requirement. The average daily driven mileage (d_a) is calculated by multiplying the daily mileage by the probabilistic distribution of driving at each instant $g(t)$. . Additionally, EVs can run in a range of electric-to-combustion-mode ratios; the amount of pure electrical mileage at particular time is determined by incorporating (λ). For the jth type of vehicle at instant t, the expected average daily traveled distance is thus given by:

$$d_a^j(t) = g(t) \times d_a \times \lambda^j(t) \tag{7}$$

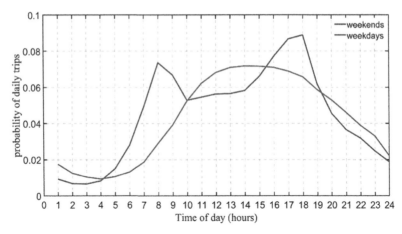

Fig. 4. Distribution of vehicle trips on weekdays and weekends

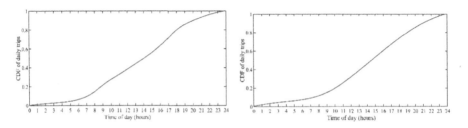

Fig. 5. Cumulative probability function for daily trips for weekdays and weekends

where $\lambda^j(t)$ represents a value between 0 and 1. Based on this, the SOC of EVs arriving at the charging station is determined using Eq. (8).

$$SOC(t) = SOC(t-1) - \left(\frac{\int_{t-1}^{t} d_{\alpha}^j(h)dh}{AER^j} \right) * 100 \qquad (8)$$

The driver's decision when to recharge or refuel the EV is governed by amount of charging or fuel left, distance between the on course charging station, destination distance left. With efficient and economic charging available, it is anticipated that drivers will prefer electric mode most of the time. Therefore, it is assumed in this study that they start trying to charge their EV batteries once it reaches its pre-decided threshold level. The EV start charging at battery's SOC δ_b^j for the instant t_b^j. The EV keeps charging until the battery's SOC is reached δ_f^j at the instant t_f^j. The initial SOC δ_b^j and final SOC δ_f^j is based on the preferences of the EV owners. The owner of the EV and the charging levels will then determine how long it takes to charge $t_f^j - t_b^j$. As a result, the energy supplied to EV_j at instant t equals

$$E_a^j(t) = L^j \times \Delta, \quad t_b^j \le t \le t_f^j \qquad (9)$$

where L^j and Δ represent the EV$_j$'s charge level (kW) and charging duration (h), respectively. During the charging interval, the anticipated value of the vehicle charging requirement is equal to

$$\left\langle E_a^j(t) \right\rangle = E_a^j(t) \times F(d_a) \tag{10}$$

The estimated EV_j demand at time t is calculated as follows:

$$\left\langle E^j(t) \right\rangle = \sum_a E_a^j(t) \times F(d_a) \tag{11}$$

$$E(t) = \sum_{j=1}^{n} E^j(t) \tag{12}$$

It is expected that there are enough charging stations available to accommodate EVs whenever they arrive at the station.

3 Methodology

In order to determine the power demand patterns of rapid charging EVs, a scenario-based algorithm is developed. This study uses Monte Carlo Simulation to create a comprehensive driver mobility-based fast charging demand estimation model [15]. As input, statistical information from NHTS is utilized to calculate battery capacity, departure timings, trip distances, parking times at various locations, energy consumption rates, and travel speeds. The simulation makes the premise that all vehicles are charged every day at random locations, including charging stations, homes, and workplaces. As a result, in this work an aggregate charging demand is generated. Figure 6 presents a thorough explanation of the charging demand estimation model's algorithm. The simulated outcome shows the overall power demand brought on by EVs.

4 Results and Discussions

In this work, load demand for fast charging station is estimated. A fleet of 500 vehicles is considered for the study and it is assumed that the vehicles return to charging station to charge their vehicles up to 100% SOC every day. Total 500 vehicles are categorized into five different types as per Table I. SOC of EV's battery is considered to take random values between 10% to 95%. Similarly, the initial SOC of the battery is randomly selected between 10% to 20% and final SOC is randomly considered between 70% to 95%. Simulation is carried out in MATLAB [16] with 8 GB RAM processor. Number of Scenarios are varied in Monte Carlo Simulation from 500 to 10000 to observe the convergence of the simulation. Expected charging demand is simulated for confidence intervals varying from 85% to 99%. Therefore, instead of getting point estimation, estimation interval is generated. Figures 7 and 8 show the anticipated EV charging demand curves for a workday and a weekend, respectively.

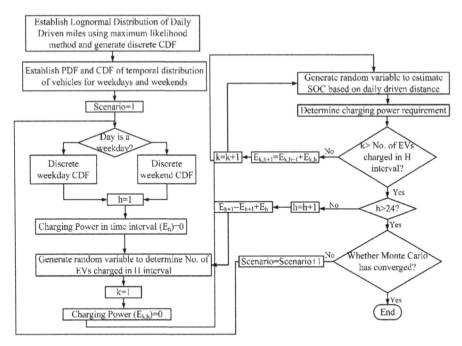

Fig. 6. Flowchart to estimate stochastic EV charging load demand

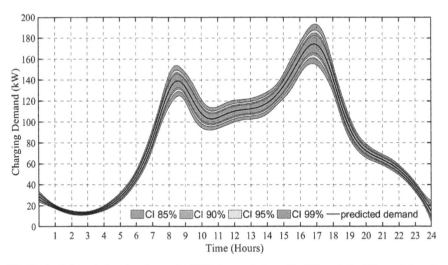

Fig. 7. Anticipated charging demand of EVs for weekday with different Confidence Intervals

The highest demand for charging typically takes place during the morning hours (07:00–09:00) and evening hours (16:00–18:00) on weekdays, as shown in Fig. 7 while only one peak is observed for the weekend. Further, variation of 40 kW is anticipated during evening peak hours for the weekday for 99% confidence interval. This estimation interval is low for morning peak hours for the peak day. This is expected as the majority of the population comes back to their respective destination during this hour and also venture out for carrying out the errands. The width of the estimation band reduces with the confidence interval. The confidence interval of 99% implies that 99% of all the charging demands will lie in this band.

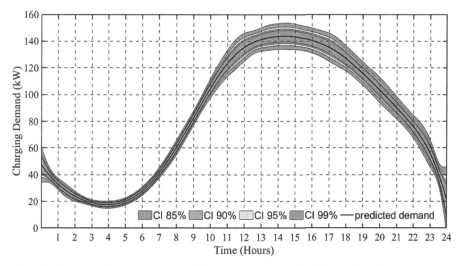

Fig. 8. Expected charging demand of EVs for weekends with different Confidence Intervals

For the weekends, width of the estimation band is around 20 kW for the evening peak hours for the weekends as per Fig. 8. Further large variation is also observed in the midnight hours. This coincides with the population being outside for leisure activities. Further, shift in peak compared to weekdays is also observed. This evening peak now lies 13:00 to 16:00 h. Based on the above results, shift in peak and different variation in charging demand will be observed for weekdays and weekends.

5 Conclusions

The EV charging demand is simulated accounting for uncertain factors like weekdays-weekends, types of vehicle, AERs, driving patterns, user behavior, energy demand, initial and final SOC. These uncertainties are incorporated by establishing transportation survey based probability distribution functions. Monte Carlo simulations is run to generate the charging scenarios and the interval-based estimation of charging demand is developed. It is inferred that multiple peaks occur for weekday while a single peak for weekends or holidays. Further, width of the estimation band is more for weekday compared to weekend implying more uncertainty for the weekdays. Also, the charging demand is more for weekdays and shift in evening peak demand is observed for the weekends. This approach accounts for the inherent variability and uncertainty associated with EV charging behaviours, enabling a more accurate estimation of prediction intervals of the charging demand. In future, further uncertain factors like weather data, electricity pricing and special occasions will be utilized to develop more accurate interval-based estimation EV charging profile. Also, validation of the model with the help of field measurement will be attempted.

References

1. Simpson, M., Markel, T.: Plug-In Electric Vehicle Fast Charge Station Operational Analysis With Integrated Renewables (2012). http://www.nrel.gov/docs/fy12osti/53914.pdf. Accessed 29 May 2018
2. Bibra, E.M., et al.: Global EV outlook 2022: Securing supplies for an electric future (2022)
3. SAE Electric Vehicle and Plug in Hybrid Electric Vehicle Conductive Charge Coupler J1772_201710. SAE International (2017)
4. Almutairi, A., Alyami, S.: Load profile modeling of plug-in electric vehicles: realistic and ready-to-use benchmark test data. IEEE Access 9, 59637–59648 (2021)
5. Uimonen, S., Lehtonen, M.: Simulation of electric vehicle charging stations load profiles in office buildings based on occupancy data. Energies 13(21), 5700 (2020)
6. Tang, D., Wang, P.: Probabilistic modeling of nodal charging demand based on spatial-temporal dynamics of moving electric vehicles. IEEE Trans. Smart Grid 7(2), 627–636 (2016)
7. Storti Gajani, G., Bascetta, L., Gruosso, G.: Data-driven approach to model electrical vehicle charging profile for simulation of grid integration scenarios. IET Electr. Syst. Transp. 9(4), 168–175 (2019)
8. Yang, W., Xiang, Y., Liu, J., Gu, C.: Agent-based modeling for scale evolution of plug-in electric vehicles and charging demand. IEEE Trans. Power Syst. 33(2), 1915–1925 (2018)
9. Ebrahimi, M., Rastegar, M.: Data-driven charging load estimation of behind-the-meter V2G-capable EVs. IEEE Trans. Ind. Appl. Early Access. (2020). https://doi.org/10.1109/TIA.2020.3012111
10. Sadhukhan, A., Ahmad, Md.S., Sivasubramani, S.: Optimal allocation of EV charging stations in a radial distribution network using probabilistic load modeling. IEEE Trans. Intell. Transp. Syst. 23(8), 11376–11385 (2021)
11. Ul-Haq, A., Cecati, C., El-Saadany, E.: Probabilistic modeling of electric vehicle charging pattern in a residential distribution network. Electr. Power Syst. Res. 157, 126–133 (2018)
12. Tehrani, N.H., Wang, P.: Probabilistic estimation of plug-in electric vehicles charging load profile. Electr. Power Syst. Res. 124, 133–143 (2015)
13. Moon, H., Park, S.Y., Jeong, C., Lee, J.: Forecasting electricity demand of electric vehicles by analyzing consumers' charging patterns. Transp. Res. D Transp. Environ. 62, 64–79 (2018)
14. U.S. Department of Transportation: National Household Travel Survey 2009 (2009). http://nhts.ornl.gov/
15. Harrison, R.L.: Introduction to monte carlo simulation. In: AIP Conference Proceedings, vol. 1204, no. 1, pp. 17–21. American Institute of Physics (2010)
16. MATLAB version 7.10 (R2014a), The Mathworks, Inc., Natick, Massachusetts (2014)

Author Index

Printed in the United States
by Baker & Taylor Publisher Services